ORGASMO ADULT ESCAPES FROM THE ZOO

by Franca Rame
and Dario Fo
adapted by Estelle Parsons

BROADWAY PLAY PUBLISHING INC
224 E 62nd St, NY, NY 10065
www.broadwayplaypub.com
info@broadwayplaypub.com

First printing: July 1985
Second printing: June 1988
Third printing: April 1998

ISBN: 978-0-88145-028-6

Book design: Marie Donovan
Printed on recycled acid-free paper and bound in the
USA

CONTENTS

Dario Fo: A Chronology iv
Estelle Parsons v
PROLOGUE 1
A WOMAN ALONE 5
MAMMA FRICCHETONA (THE FREAK
MOMMY) 21
WAKING UP 31
WE ALL HAVE THE SAME STORY 37
DIALOGUE FOR A SINGLE VOICE 46
MEDEA PROLOGUE 52
MEDEA 56
MONOLOGUE OF A WHORE IN A LUNATIC
ASYLUM 61
IT HAPPENS TOMORROW 68
Adaptor's note & original production history 72

DARIO FO: A CHRONOLOGY

1926: Born in the province of Varese, North Italy.
Attends art school in Milan and studies architecture
at Politecnico.
1952-4: Writes and performs monologues for radio
which transfer to the theater. Takes part in satirical
revues and meets with censorship.
1957-59: Produces classical farces working with Franca
Rame, his wife and close collaborator. They include
ONE WAS NUDE AND ONE WORE TAILS and THE
VIRTUOUS BURGLAR.
1959-67: Writes and produces a series of comedies for
the bourgeois theater, including ARCHANGELS
DON'T PLAY PINBALL. He has difficulty because of
his criticism of bourgeois society.

In 1962 Fo is asked to produced the popular television
program *Canzonissima*. The show is heavily censored
because of its satirical content. Fo and Rame refuse to
accept the cuts.

In 1966 he produces and works on CI RAGIONO E
CANTO, which draws on popular and folk songs.
1968-70: Together with Rame sets up the Nuova Scena
company, which breaks with the bourgeois theater and
works through the cultural institutions of the Italian
Communist Party. In this period MISTERO BUFFO was
created.
1970-74: Fo and Rame break with the Communist Party,
which they consider too reformist, and set up the
theatrical collective La Comune. In the 1970-71

season they put on ACCIDENTAL DEATH OF
AN ANARCHIST and CAN'T PAY? WON'T PAY!
1977: Rame and Fo publish ALL HOME, BED AND
CHURCH, a volume of monologues for female voices.
1983: THE OPEN COUPLE by Fo and Rame looks at
the place of women in society.
1984: ELIZABETH, ALMOST BY CHANCE A
WOMAN, set at the court of the aging Elizabeth I.
1986: AN ORDINARY DAY and a new edition of
THE OPEN COUPLE are published under the title
FEMALE PARTS, by Fo and Rame.
1989: THE POPE AND WITCH looks at the problems
of drugs and contraception. TWENTY-FIVE
MONOLOGUES OF A WOMAN (English title
A WOMAN ALONE AND OTHER PLAYS) assembles
texts by Rame and Fo on the theme of woman's fate in
society.
1990: ZITTI STIAMO PRECIPITANDO looks at AIDS.
1991: Rame's PARLIAMO DI DONNE and Fo's JOHAN
PADA A LA DESCOVERTA DE LA AMERICHE, a
worm's eye view of the "discovery" of America.
1997: Dario Fo is awarded the Nobel Prize for literature.

ESTELLE PARSONS

Estelle Parsons was described by Frank Rich in *The New
York Times* as having "an artistic impulse that is both
passionate and rare." An Academy Award winner,
Miss Parsons has distinguished herself in all major
areas of the entertainment field. The day of her arrival
in New York City from Marblehead, Massachusetts,
with a B A degree from Connecticut College for Women
and a year of law school experience, she was hired as
one of the eight people who put together the
N B C *Today Show* for national television. She then

became the first woman to do political news reporting for a television network.

She made her professional acting debut at the Cherry Lane Theater in William Hanley's MRS DALLY HAS A LOVER, for which she won a Theater World Award for Most Promising Newcomer. She made her Broadway debut in HAPPY HUNTING with Ethel Merman. Other New York appearances include MISS MARGARIDA'S WAY by Brazilian Roberto Athayde, which marked the debut of a South American playwright on Broadway. She also starred on Broadway in Tennessee Williams' SEVEN DESCENTS OF MYRTLE, Paul Zindel's AND MISS REARDON DRINKS A LITTLE and Alan Ayckbourn's THE NORMAN CONQUESTS.

The year after she won the Academy Award for *Bonnie and Clyde*, she was nominated for a second Oscar for Paul Newman's *Rachel, Rachel*. Other films include *I Never Sang for My Father*; *I Walk the Line* with Gregory Peck; Woody Allen's *Don't Drink the Water*; Melvin Van Peebles' *Watermelon Man*; *For Pete's Sake* with Barbra Streisand; *The Lemon Sisters*, produced by Diane Keaton; Warren Beatty's film *Dick Tracy*; *Boys on the Side* with Whoopi Goldberg; Disney's *That Darned Cat*; and as Queen Margaret in Al Pacino's *Looking for Richard*.

Her television credits include her role as Mother Bev on *Roseanne*; several appearances on *All in the Family* and *Archie's Place*; *Open Admissions*; *The U F O Incident* with James Earl Jones; her role as Bess Truman in *Backstairs at the White House*; *Terror on the Beach*; and Hallmark's *The Love Letter*.

She is a member of the Society of Stage Directors and Choreographers and the League of Professional Theater Women. She is currently Artistic Director of The Actor's Studio in Manhattan.

PROLOGUE

(This prologue is "warm up" material and should be paraphrased in performance to achieve its purpose.)

Good evening, and welcome to ADULT ORGASM ESCAPES FROM THE ZOO (ORGASMO ADULTO ESCAPES FROM THE ZOO), which is an entertainment about women and their sexual situation. It was born in Milano, Italia, at the Palazzina Liberty in 1977 in support of the Italian Women's Movement. It was written by Franca Rame and Dario Fo and performed by Franca Rame. Its success carried it all over Italy and finally all over the world.

The "protagonista assoluto," or principal character, of this entertainment is man—to put it better, his sexuality! That sexuality is not present "in the flesh" but it is always here, among us ... big, awful, hovering over us ... it squashes us! We women, oh, it's so long that we've been fighting for our freedom—equality with men, social equality, sexual equality. We've made some progress socially but with the "sexual equality" we have not. We will never be equal with men in that area. Too many taboos! We are born with them, they are there before we are born. Inhibitions about our behavior. Even in language itself. I, for example, and I'm pretty uninhibited here, in public, in front of everyone here, I could not bring myself to say the name ... first name or last name, of that thing there, the male organ. I couldn't bring myself to say it, maybe only in a curse, in a rage, so I would curse, "Goddamn my inhibitions about the prick!" That's about all I could do. I believe with time we'll overcome the language problem. I'm talking about my generation, because the younger generations don't seem to have this difficulty. Whether their language is rebellion against their parents or society, it makes them feel avant-garde, free, superior. But the fact is we all remain prisoners of the culture of the c——the male organ.

Let's face it, sexual equality is a utopian dream even if we want it because of an anatomical reality. Man is made in

a way that is different from us ... he possesses a tail ... yes, a
little tail, the devil has it in back, man has it in front ... a
lively, dynamic, animated tail! We women are just apes
without tails! There's a famous book written about this! And
we women without tails must resign ourselves. He with his
mischievous tail has a living miracle! What a miracle ...
erection! A miracle, I remind you, that can occur in any at-
mospheric conditions, in damp weather, while moving
around, out of doors, or indoors ... in the wind, under
water. Men are very proud of their sexuality. Since classical
times they've given epic, supercilious, grandiloquent names
to their organ. The PREPUCE, the GLANS, the PHALLUS!
These names belong in a tragedy by Euripides. I've jotted
something down here.

CAME THE MIGHTIEST ERMIONE
ERECT BEFORE HIM ARMED,
HIS HELMET LIFTED FROM HIS BROW
PREPUCE, INDOMITABLE
ADJACENT HIS BROTHER GLANS,
     RESPLENDENT
FOMENTING THE GALLOPING SCROTUM
HOISTING BETWEEN THEM THE PENIS
FOR THE HEROIC CHARGE

Beautiful, no? Man elevated his member to his image and
likeness. It is him, his thing, his power ... the power
assoluto! If we think a little, the world does not revolve
around the United States ... or Russia: The world revolves
around the Grand Phallsa! The real tiger, not the paper one,
is what it is! Notwithstanding its modest proportions ... ah, I
knew it, you've taken offense! But you see, it's not its size as
you've been erroneously taught ... to give it heroic proportions. "He's really hung!" "What a schlong!" "Nine in-
ches and loaded!" It's not its size, I was saying, but its in-
trinsic quality, its imaginative behavior, the way it thinks.
What are you laughing at? Yes, it thinks, gentlemen! It has
a brain, it thinks, believe me! You know we say about someone foolish or stupid, "That prick!" We are lacking the

proper respect. In ancient time that term was reserved for kings, for rulers, for the most powerful! There were statues of the PHALLUS, paintings, engravings, works of art! You can see them in museums all over the world. Then it began to degenerate ... this respect for the phallus ... the word was used for politicians, presidents, and finally was given to the common man with his taste for irreverence, which is properly his right. Now this respectful title has become invective and we only see it represented visually. Where? In *Screw* magazine. But looking at it another way, it's a revolutionary turnabout ... a victory of the have-nots over the haves ... now anyone can be a prick! Even a woman! A true social victory!

Excuse me, I digress! Where was I? Ah, yes, Euripides "HOISTING BETWEEN THEM THE PENIS FOR THE HEROIC CHARGE!" Inspiring isn't it? Now let's try to compose a classical poem built around the words we have to describe the sexual parts of the female anatomy:

CAME THE MOST SWEET BRISIDE
EXTENDING HERSELF
AND WITH HER, LOVER OF PELIDUS,
THE INFURIATED CLITORIS!

Clitoris is horrible, disgusting ... so is VULVA, VAGINA, OVARY, they sound awful ... what can you create with them? Ecch! Just the thought of a poem using VULVA makes my skin crawl ... perhaps only in some passage of Dante, in the Inferno:

A GIANT WILD BEAST APPROACHES AT A
GALLOP
HAIRY AND HORRIBLE, GNASHING ITS
TEETH
SUDDENLY TERRA FIRMA TREMBLED
A VULVA, SAVAGE
SEIZES ME BY THE THROAT!

Vagina then ... you can only slip on a vagina, "I broke my leg slipping on a vagina peel," or in a horror story:

BATS CIRCLING IN THE DUSK
VAGINAS CROAKING IN THE SWAMP
IT WAS THE MOMENT TO DEPOSIT THE
  OVARIES
A TREMENDOUS UTERUS ROSE INTO THE
  NIGHT
ALL THE SPERMATAZOA DIED OF FRIGHT

No, we're not so good for poems!

The pieces are comic, grotesque, on purpose. First of all because we women have been crying for two thousand years. So let's laugh now, even at ourselves. And also because a certain gentleman of the theatre who knew a lot, a certain Moliere, used to say: When you go to the theatre and see a tragedy, you identify, empathize, cry, cry, cry, then go home and say, "What a good cry I had tonight," and you have a good night's sleep. The social significance went by like water over glass. But for us to provoke you to laughter —and it's always Moliere who speaks—you have to have a brain, you have to be alert ... to laugh you throw open your mouth and also your brain and into your brain are hammered the nails of reason. We hope tonight that someone will go home with his or her head nailed down.

A WOMAN ALONE

(*Livingroom of middle-class house.* WOMAN *dancing with laundry basket. Ironing board, center. On it, iron, telephone, radio (blaring).* WOMAN *sets down basket and irons, facing audience. Speaks to imaginary woman across the alley.*)

WOMAN: Signora ... Signora. Good morning ... When did you come to live right across from my house? ... I didn't see anyone move in ... Yes. I thought it was still empty. I'm happy ... (*Half shouting*) I said I'm happy ... you can't hear me? Ah, yes, you're right ... the radio ... I'll turn it off, right away. ... (*Does so*). I'm so sorry but when I'm in the house alone if I don't play the radio—loud —there comes to me this desire to kill myself.

In this room (*Goes to door*) I always have the stereo playing. (*Opens door—we hear music.*) Hear it? (*Closes door*) In the kitchen the cassette player. (*Opens door*) Hear that? (*Closes door*) So into whatever room I go, I have company. (*Goes to board and begins to brush man's jacket, put on buttons, etc.*) No ... in the bedroom, no, how could you think such a thing? No, I have the television on in there ... always, yes, yes ... as loud as it will play. Right now they're televising a Mass, a high Mass ... in Polish ... what a language! The language of the Pope! You can't understand one word ... Yes I like it even when its not danceable ... as long as it's music ... the sound of it keeps me company ... and you, how do you keep yourself company? Ah, you have a son! How lucky ... How stupid—I have a son ... No—I have two. Pardon me. I forgot one in the excitement of talking to you ... but they don't keep me company. The little girl is big with her own boyfriends and girlfriends ... The little boy, though, is always home with me, but not even he keeps me company ... He sleeps! Sleeps all the time! Makes his poo-poo! Eats and snores ... he snores ... like an old man! But I'm not complaining, I'm happy in my house. ... I'm not missing a thing ... my husband doesn't let me go without. ... I have everything! I have ... God. I have so much ... I've got a refrigerator!

... Si, I know everyone in the world ha.; a refrigerator (*Very grand*) but mine makes round ice cubes!! I've got a washing machine, 24 cycles!! ... Washes and dries ... dries!? ... Sometimes I have to wet everything to be able to iron it ... it's too dry! I have a wok, a vegetable juice extractor, a blender "Waring." Music in every room. What more could I want? I'm only a woman, after all! ... Yes, I had one, by the hour. But she ran away, escaped; then another one came, she quit, escaped like the other one. All the maids deserted me. ... What? ... No, it's not my fault. (*Embarrassed*) It's my brother-in-law. ... What? He touches them. He's always touching them! Right there! ... He's crippled ... Pervert? ... I don't know. ... I only know that he wanted something from those girls and they—quite rightly —slapped him down. I'd like to see what you would do, dear Signora, there you are busy, busy, busy with your Hoover and CHICAHCHICHACHICATRAAHCKETAY! he slips his hand up under ... and you should see that hand! Lucky he only has the one. ... But no, how could you think that? ... An accident (*During this she sits and sews by the window, talking across alley.*), an automobile accident. ... Imagine, so young, only 33, just like Jesus, and smashed to pieces! He's all plastered up from head to foot; they plastered him in a sitting position so he'd be more comfortable. ... They've only left a little hole to breathe and eat, but to speak, no, he can't, mumbles only sometimes ... you can't understand a word! His eyes were okay, so they left those out ... then they left out ... they left out that touching hand ... then there's something else that was okay ... that *is* okay. (*She can't go on—embarrassed.*) How can I say it ... we've known each other such a short time, I wouldn't like you to think badly of me ... let's see ... he's okay (*Looks down*) there. He is so okay there, Signora! Too okay! He always wants to ... you know? ... Yes, he has other interests. He reads, he reads a great deal ... Keeps informed ... PORNO COMICS. His room is full of disgusting magazines, the ones with the naked women in certain positions! Uncomfortable. If you ask me, those poor girls, after those pictures, they need to be plastered up like my brother-in-law! ... Pieces of anatomical flesh. ... Close-ups in full color ... Just like the poster of the cow down at the butcher's! ... I tell you. When I happen to have one of those magazines in my hand, then, at noon, I go in to cook the steak, I want to throw up ... And, so, since all the maids have left, I take care of my brother-in-law myself, you know I do it for my husband ... it's his brother, after all. ... What are you saying? (*Angry*) Me? No! Me he respects! With me, he's a different person! With me, he asks permission always! (*Phone rings*) Oh, that must be my husband ... he always calls me now ... Pardon me a moment ... (*Picks up phone*) Pronto? ... What? Yes ... what. ... Fuck off, you big shit! (*Slams down phone. She's furious, looks out window, and smiles apologetically.*) I NEVER SWEAR. Please excuse me, but when you have to, you have to. (*Starts working again, nervously.*) No, no that wasn't my husband, it was a different person. ... No, I don't know who. ... It was a dirty phone call. He calls up one, two, ... a thousand times a day ... says disgusting things to me ... there are no such words. ... I tried to look them up in the dictionary. ... They're not there! ... Sick? You know, I already have one sick man in my house ... I can't take care of all the dirty old men in Italy, you know? (*Phone rings*) There he is again. This time I'm not giving him a chance. (*Picks up phone*) Pronto, you pig! You'd better stop calling because this phone is tapped by the police and if you ... (*Changes tone completely*) Ciao ... (*Covers phone, turns to window.*) it's my husband! (*Speaks in phone*) No. I wasn't talking to you, dear. ... I thought it was ... there's a man who keeps calling up ... he asks for you ... he uses terrible language ... he's furious with you ... he says you owe him money ... So I thought I'd threaten him with the police. (*Changes tone —completely amazed! Grows more amazed!*) I'm at home! Aldo, I swear I'm at home! Excuse me, what number did you call? And who answered. ... I am not out! How could I go out when you've locked me in the house? (*Turns to window*) Signora, look at my husband, he's nuts ... (*In telephone*) No, I'm not talking to someone else. ... Yes. I said Signora ... but when I talk to myself I call myself "Signora" ... No, there's no one else in the house. ... Yes, there is your brother

but he's not here, he's in there looking at his movies. ... Yes,
the baby's asleep. ... Yes, I've fed him. ... Yes, he did his
pipi. (*Snide*) Yes, so did your brother. (*Tries to control herself.*)
But who's angry. ... I said, take it easy, everyone in the
house has pipied. ... Ciao, okay ... no, no, I'm happy ...
I'm happy, Aldo, I'm very happy. (*Getting more nervous*) I'm
here ironing and laughing. (*Shouting*) I'm happy. (*Puts down
receiver, screeches, growls at phone ... looks out window, serious and
tense, then makes a big silent smile. Gets control of herself.*) You see!
I have to lie to him! ... Uh, no. He doesn't know about the
dirty phone calls. ... If I tell him, he'll blame me. ... Uh, I
know it's not my fault, but he tells me that they keep calling
because they hear I get all upset so they get more excited!
He'll probably end up taking out the telephone! ... Already
he's locked me in ... LOCKS ME IN! Every morning when
he goes to work. ... Shopping? He does it. ... (*Resumes ironing*) What if something happens, he telephones all day ...
what could possibly happen in my house. ... We're such a
quiet family ... (*Stops ironing, her gaze goes higher. Tries to cover
her breasts—left with a bib; right—the iron at the proper moment;
loud voice.*) You know I can see you. (*To her neighbor*) Pardon
me a moment. (*Looking higher*) It's useless to hide. You know
I see your binoculars shining in the sun. (*Puts iron on breast
and takes off quickly; to neighbor.*) Oh my God, I've pressed my
breast!! No, you can't see him ... it's a window above you
... (*To audience*) So we also have the peeping Tom wanting to
get into the act today! ... See, a poor woman can't even do a
little ironing in her own house in her negligee ... because of
him I should do my ironing in my fur coat. (*Shouting at the
peeping Tom.*) Is that it? ... And a hood over my head. ...
And some skis! ... And there's not even any snow in here!
I'll get all smashed up like my brother-in-law! (*To neighbor*)
The police? No, I won't call them. What for? They arrive,
they question me, they want to know was I naked or dressed
in my own house. ... If I provoked the peeping Tom with
erotic dances and then I get arrested. I get arrested for
obscene behavior on private premises exposed to public
view! No, no ... I'll do it myself. (*Takes very large gun from wall

and points it at peeping Tom's window—shouting.) I'll murder
you! (*Disappointed*) He escaped. (*To peeping Tom*) You see the
rifle, you run away! Coward! Blind son of a binocularist!
(*Points gun at neighbor. To neighbor.*) I make you laugh? I'm
crazy? (*Puts down gun, returns to ironing.*) Better be crazy than
do what I was doing before. Every two months I'd swallow a
whole bottle of NoDoz, also all the round pills I could find in
the medicine chest. The ExLax, even the worm pills for the
dog ... I was so desperate!! Once I slit my wrists ... look, the
scars are still there. See? (*Shows her wrists.*) No, Signora, I'm
sorry, but the story of the slit wrists, it is not possible for me
to tell. It is private, intimate. I wouldn't feel right. ... We
know each other such a short time ... (*Changes tone completely*)
Shall I tell you? ... No, no. I just had a desire to confide in
your apartment house! Perhaps it would be good for me. ...
I could get it off my chest. It's a sad story! Well ... it's all
because of a boy ... fifteen years younger than me ... who
looked even younger than that ... shy, clumsy ... sweet ...
delicate ... to make love with him would be like ... incest! Incest!! I did it! Did what? The incest, I made love with the
boy and the most terrible thing? I wasn't ashamed of it ... in
fact, I was happy! I was singing all day but at night ... at
night, no I cried ... "You are depraved," I told myself.
(*Honking is heard*) Pardon, that's my brother-in-law calling
me with his horn ... one moment, I'll be right back ... (*Sticks
her head through left door.*) What is it? ... Be quiet for a minute,
I'm talking to a lady. (*Phones rings, closes door, and runs to
answer phone.*) Pronto ... what is it, Aldo? (*Turns to window*)
Yes, yes, I'm listening to you ... if who comes? The man
about the money? ... (*Almost to herself*) And who is the man
about the money?! Ah, that man who always telephones. ...
So what if he does? ... I'm locked in, you know, it would be
difficult to get him in through the keyhole. Ah, I should pretend I'm not home ... turn off the radio, the stereo, the
television. ... Oh, whatever you want, at your service,
General! Listen, I'll do even more for you. I'll go into the
bathroom, dive into the toilet and pull the chain. ... What?
Drop dead! (*Bangs phone, is furious.*) He says when he gets

home he's going to smash my face in ... Me? My husband
hit me? ... He always does!! (*Works again*) He says he does it
because he loves me, he adores me! How I'm still a baby, he
has to protect me ... and to protect me better he locks me in
the house like a dimwitted chicken. I mean, normal chickens
aren't outstandingly intelligent, are they, so imagine a
stupid one!! He beats me up ... and then, all of a sudden, he
wants to make love! Yes, love! And he doesn't care if I'm
ready, if I want to! Always ready I have to be, always ready!
Like Nescafe! Washed, perfumed, shaved, undone, eager
but silent ... It's enough that I breathe and make a little
squeal every so often to let him know it's good! The fact is I
don't feel ... do you know I never have a ... (*Is very embarrassed,
doesn't find the right word—the neighbor suggests it.*) Yes, that's it
... that's the word. ... That word, "that word," I never say
it, "orgasm." It's like the name of some disgusting animal
... a cross between an armadillo and an orangutang. It's like
a headline on the paper, "Adult Orgasm Escapes from
American Circus," "Nun at Zoo Attacked by Crazed
Orgasm." And when they say, "He reached an orgasm," I
see this poor guy who after a long, long run just makes the
bus on time. (*Laugh*) Ah, it has the same effect on you? ...
OR-GAAS-MM!! It's a boogey man to frighten the
children. What a word. With all the names there are, why
couldn't they call it for example, "chair"? Yes, "chair,"
you could say, "I reached a chair." First, no one's going to
know you're doing something dirty ... second, if you're
tired, you sit down! (*Laugh*) Where was I? Ah, yes, excuse
me, but this business about orgasm made me lose the thread
... with my husband ... I feel nothing! Nothing! Look how I
make love to my husband. (*Changes tone*) You won't tell
anyone, will you? ... Like this. (*Stiffens body like soldier at attention.*) And when he finishes, I say, "At ease." No, not out
loud, he'd hit me ... to myself ... I talk to myself. "At ease."
I don't know why I don't feel anything. It might be because
I didn't have much sexual experience ... I only had two ...
my husband, that doesn't count, and one other when I was
young ... I was ten and he was twelve. What a lamebrain!

Let's hope he grew out of it ... We didn't know anything
about it ... we only knew babies came from the tummy. ...
No. I didn't feel anything. Not a thing! Only very, very sore
here. (*Indicates belly button*) Yes, here ... belly button ... and
yes, because we thought that was it, the place for love ... and
so he with his thing—push, push! My belly button was all
red I don't know how long. My mother thought I had the
measles! Poor thing. ... To my husband, this story about the
belly button, no, I didn't tell him. ... No, because maybe
after ten years when we had a fight, "Shut up, what about
the time with the belly button—you cheated on me." No, I
kept quiet. ... I told the priest. ... I confessed. ... He told me
not to do it again. Afterwards I grew up. ... No, I didn't
have any other sexual experiences. ... No, I didn't like that
belly button experience. ... I grew up, I got engaged, my
girlfriends told me ... my wedding day I was so excited I was
singing at the top of my lungs. ... No, not out loud, inside ...
I do everything inside. In the church I was singing inside ...
Here comes love, oho ohoo ... here comes love. (*Changes tone
completely*) Instead, what came, my husband! I was so disappointed that first time, Signora ... "How come—is that
all?" I said to myself. ... I was so disappointed that first time
... and the hundredth time! ... Find out about it? WHERE?
From whom? ... I started reading the women's magazines
and I discovered something!! (*Importantly*) I found out we
women have erogenous zones ... these are zones that are
sensitive sexually to the touch of a man ... (*Disappointed*) Ah,
you know it already. ... You know a lot, don't you? But how
many do we have? ... In this magazine there was a drawing
of a naked lady, all divided into sections. ... You know, like
those charts that you see hanging at the butcher shop, and
every erogenous zone was painted with a bright color
according to its sensitivity—very strong to weak. For example, the rump, shocking pink. And this part behind the neck
butchers call "chuck," purple. Then the filet, orange. Then
the sirloin ... ah, the sirloin is baaaddd!! The ultimate!
Special! Almost like the "loin," you know, if a man knows
how to touch it, the loin, it gives such erotic tremors you

burst! With my husband, no rump, no chuck, no sirloin ...
not even any ground round, nothing! I feel nothing! But I
resigned myself because I thought it's that way for all
women ... then I met the boy. Here's what happened. My
daughter got big, was big, and I had less to do, so I said to
my husband, "Listen, I'm tired of doing housework, I'd like
to do something intellectual, learn a language. English, for
example, then when we go to America they all speak it there
like mad all the time." He says to me, "Brava!" And he
brings to the house this university student, 26 years old.
Speaks English beautifully. So we start the lessons. Three
weeks go by and it occurs to me this boy is madly in love
with me! ... How did I know? Yes ... if when he's explaining
a word his hand should touch my hand, just brushes mine,
he would tremble all over ... he'd start stuttering the English
so you couldn't understand a word! There he'd sit, across
the table from me and I could feel the waves of love coming
at me. Vroom, vroom, vroom—it made me seasick! I wasn't
used to anyone so sensitive, only my brother-in-law's hand,
the heavy breather on the telephone, or my husband. Then I
started feeling something. I said to myself, "Uh? Uh, uh!
Ah-uh-ah," when I talk to myself I don't need many words.
I know the questions and the answers! I said to myself, "Are
you slipping towards sin?" I stopped with the English! He,
the boy, he took it very badly ... every day when I went
down to do the shopping he was there, in a doorway, waiting
for me. With his raincoat collar turned up, looking like a
young Yul Brynner and staring at me with his beautiful blue
eye. ... No, he has two eyes ... I think it sounds better that
way ... his beautiful blue eye. ... I said to him (*Speaking out of
side of mouth.*), "Go away. I'm not the woman for you ... go
away. ... I'm old enough to be your mother! Get a girl your
own age. ... (*Shrieking*) Go away!!" (*Change totally*) He got so
frightened! Then one day he did something unforgettable. I
went down as usual to do my shopping and in the doorway
he wasn't there! I was so disappointed!! "It's okay," I told
myself, "He's given up." I go into the square, down here,
and something attracts me. ... On the walls of the houses

written in enormous letters with red paint ... it was written:
"I love you, Maria," "I love you, Maria," in English so no
one understood! I ran home. "Enough, I have to forget ..."
And to forget I began to drink "Fernet Branca." Bitter!
How bitter—"Fernet Branca!" But why is it so bitter! I'd
swallow it like medicine ... and here I was with all my bit-
ternesses, the radio playing, the telephone ringing, my
brother-in-law honking. ... (*Honks*) Here we go again. (*Goes
toward left door.*) What is it? Be good now, I can't, I'm talking
to my friend. (*More honks*) Bastard! (*To neighbor*) He swears at
me with that horn. Someday I'm going to push him down
the stairs, him and his wheelchair ... all four flights ... (*To
the furious horn—she is furious.*) He has to have the last honk,
don't you! Where was I? Oh, yes, drunk on the "Fernet
Branca," no, no, not drunk ... tipsy. ... Brring—the
doorbell. Who was it? The boy's mother! Soo embarrassed!!
She says, "Signora, please don't think badly of me. I'm
desperate. My son is dying of love for you. He won't eat, he
won't sleep, he won't drink. ... Save him!! Come at least to
say hello." What should I do? I'm a mother also! I go. I go
into the boy's room ... he's in bed ... white as a sheet, thin,
sad. Soon as he sees me he bursts into tears ... then his
mother bursts into tears ... then I burst into tears ... then his
mother leaves the room. We're alone. (*Very embarrassed*) He
holds me, I hold him. Then he kisses me ... I ... kiss him ...
and then ... (*Shrieking*) "Stop!" He got so frightened like the
other time. "I have to talk to you. I'm not ashamed to tell
you. I like you so much, in fact I love you. (*Getting louder and
louder.*) I love you. I love you. I loooove you!" I hollered so
loud!! ... The Fernet Branca!! (*Still yelling*) Loove you!
(*Changing tone*) Afterwards they told me everyone in the
building rushed to the windows: "Who's in love in this
building?" "Is it someone on the fourth floor?" "No, not
here. Some other floor!" What a show!! Lucky no one
knows me there. ... (*Shouting again*) "I love you! But I can't
make love with you. I have two children, I have a husband, I
have a brother-in-law!" He then jumps out of bed, naked ...
he was so naked! He grabbed a knife that was there, put it to

his throat and said, "If you don't make love with me ... I'll
kill myself!" (*Even more embarrassed*) I'm not a murderess!
Would I sacrifice a young life to my selfishness? Never! Oh,
Signora, it was beautiful ... so delicate, oh those kisses ...
Those caresses ... you should have been there, Signora. God
bless that knife! That is how I discovered love, LOVE, is not
that business with my husband ... me on the bottom and him
on top! Brrum, brrrum, brrrum, the asphalt road banger.
Love is sweet ... so sweet ... I went back the next day, then
the day after, all the days after the days after ... What do you
mean, Signora? He was a sick boy! And when I got back to
my house I was stunned ... What, why? To get all the way to
my age to discover that it happens in real life what I thought
only happened in the movies ... My husband, seeing me so
stupid, didn't he get it in his head I was drinking? He locks
up the Fernet Branca! What a boob!! Then he got suspicious
and he had me followed without even telling me! One day
I'm here, in the boy's room ... standing there, naked ... and
he's there, standing there naked, we're just saying, "Hello.
How are you?" "Fine. And you?" The door bursts open
and in comes my husband, fully clothed! I didn't know what
to say, so I said, "Ah, is it you?" Mm-mm, Signora ... it
doesn't happen every day to be standing there naked with a
stranger, naked and your husband in his overcoat. I
shouldn't have said it! "Yes, it's meee!" He starts screaming like crazy. ... He wants to strangle the boy. ... At the
same time he wants to strangle me ... but my husband has
only two hands and even squeezing hard he couldn't do it ...
even though I was helping as much as I could ... I pushed
my neck up against the boy's. I even stopped breathing ... I
held my mouth closed ... then all by itself my nose started
breathing ... I've got an independent nose!! In came his
mother, his sister, his grandmother. ... I'm here naked like a
huge worm with my independent nose. I ran into the bathroom, locked myself in ... I took a razor that was there: cutta, cutta, cutta, cutta ... I cut every vein I have. I found
them. Here's one: Cut! Another one: Cut! What a slashing.
We have so many veins. I cut them lengthwise ... it is, to die

sooner ... But my husband wanted to kill me himself. Personally, he battered down the door with his shoulders. ... When he saw me there covered with blood ... red! I have such bright red blood ... I looked like Dracula's Christmas dinner. He says, "I'm not going to kill you anymore. I'm taking you to the hospital." He wrapped me in a beautiful blanket, so his car wouldn't get dirty. ... He took me to the hospital ... and then he forgave me. ... He was very generous. But since that day, he has kept me locked up here. ... Certainly to lock up a person ... I know is prohibited by law ... the police? Is your husband a cop? I cannot call the police. ... Because if they come here, the story of the boy comes out. ... You can be sure we'd have a legal separation. ... You can be sure my husband would take the children and in exchange, you can be sure, he'd leave me his sex-crazed brother-in-law! No, no, look ... I (*Phone rings*) Pronto! (*Low voice*) Darling ... why are you telephoning me? (*Shouts to neighbor*) It's the boy! (*Returns to intimate tone.*) I beg you ... you mustn't telephone anymore! How can I meet you, if I'm locked in the house. ... You're coming to open it? With what? ... Don't do a thing like that to me. ... Hello, hello. ... (*To neighbor*) He hung up! He's crazy, he's crazy! He says he's coming here to open ... with a bent nail? ... Yes, I know he can't get it open, but how will I look if one of the tenants passes by and sees a stranger picking at my lock with a bent nail! (*Knock at the door.*) Oh ... he's already here. (*Goes to front door.*) Go away, I'm expecting my husband ... (*Changes tone*) Who are you? ... Money? What money? (*To neighbor*) God, what a mess. ... It's that man for the cash, the creditor. (*To door*) There's no one in the house. ... Yes, I am here but. ... I'm the maid ... Yes, I said my husband, but my husband is the cook. ... No, the family are not home. They've gone for a cruise ... by automobile ... Listen, I have my orders: not to open the door; not to talk; not to play the radio or the stereo ... and besides all that I can't open it because I do not have the key. ... (*Aside*) Oh God, what have I said ... (*To creditor*) I don't have the key because ... they've locked me in ... my mistress thinks I steal ... and so ... No, don't worry. I won't

starve, I have a life-saving kit ... The police? Why do you
want to call the police? (*To herself*) He must be related to that
signora there ... (*To creditor*) Mister ... Mister. ... (*Coming to
window*) If he's gone, he's gone to call the police. ... I tell you
he's bluffing. ... He's trying to scare me. ... (*Knocking on
door*) Knocking ... who's it going to be, Signora, the creditor,
the police, the crazy boy? I'm not answering for anyone. ...
(*Insistent knocking*) Could it be the police? (*Loud voice shouts:
Maria, Maria.*) My husband! (*Goes to door*) Aldo ... why are
you knocking. ... Okay, the bell's broken, but you have the
key, open that door. ... You lost your key? Oh, mamma!
What will become of me? I'm going to starve to death,
buried alive, me, my baby, that hand. What a way to die!
(*To husband*) Listen, your friend's been here, that one about
the money. He's gone to call the police. No, I didn't talk to
him. I'm not stupid! He talked to the maid. ... What maid?
We don't have a maid? Certainly we have a maid! We have
a maid, a nurse, a baby sitter, a cleaning woman, a wash
woman, and a screwing machine! ... No, I'm not hysterical,
or crazy. ... I'll be glad if the police come and everything
will be over. ... Yes, go away and never come back! (*Furious,
tries to find a word to hurt her husband.*) Cross-eyed! (*Hears what
she said, comes back to table depressed—to neighbor.*) With all the
bad words I know the one time I need one: cross-eyed! He's
got 20/20 vision! Well! What a fool I made of myself! But I
said it to him. (*Baby cries*) The baby. ... (*Scared*) Signora, he
cried, the baby ... I'm so frightened. He's never cried since
he was born! (*Exit door—left—bedroom.*) What are you doing
here in my bedroom. ... You filthy brute, you woke up my
baby just to get me in here. ... What are you doing. ... Stop.
Don't grab at me! (*Baby cries*) Be good, baby, be good!
(*Telephone rings*) Disgraceful pig! You've ripped my
Hollywood negligee. I'm coming, look at it. ... Just wait till
your brother comes back, you'll see. ... (*Enters with ripped
gown.*) If he ever comes back ... (*Answers phone*) Pronto. ...
Listen, that's enough. Look, if you dare say those disgusting
things someday I am going to forget myself—I'll put ... a
bomb in this telephone! I'll blow up your gums!! Dirty

bastard ... you should be ashamed of yourself! I am a mother! How would you like it if someone said the revolting things that you say to me to your old white-haired mamma, sitting with her knitting by the fire. ... Ah, silence! The heavy breathing stops. ... I found the magic word, the magic word that beats in the heart of every Italian: Mamma! (*Pause, puts down phone.*) He's an orphan! (*Hurls invective at phone.*) Pig, bastard, shit!! (*To neighbor*) Signora, see what my brother-in-law has done to me, he's gotten to where he wakes up the baby ... (*Calling*) Signora ... Signora ... (*Baby begins to cry—in despair*) She's gone. ... (*Looks higher*) To compensate the peeping Tom is back. (*Speaks to left door.*) Be good, honeybunch (*Levels gun*), Mamma's going to show you how to kill a peeping Tom ... (*Knock on front door—to peeping Tom.*) Stay there, I'll be right back. (*Goes to door*) Who is it. ... Please, go away. ... I'm expecting my husband, the police, and also a creditor. ... (*Noise at keyhole*) Don't you dare touch my keyhole with that nail ... you'll never get it open ... (*Noise of lock clicking.*) It's clicking, oh God, it's open. ... No, you won't get in. ... The chain is on. ... (*She puts on the chain.*) Help! (*Runs to table*) Signora, Signora. ... Oh, thank heaven you're back ... that crazy boy has opened the door ... No, he can't get in because I put on the chain ... Yes. I'll tell him ... (*Goes to door. Stops short, seeing hand of boy coming through door crack.*) Take that hand out of my house immediately. (*Hand remains*) What do you want? ... To shake hands? Don't you understand my husband's coming. ... (*The boy insists*) What persistence!! Okay. But hurry up. ... (*Gives her hand to hand. Boy tries to pull woman to him.*) What are you doing. ... I can't get through the crack. ... (*Baby cries*) Let me go, my baby's crying ... I have to give him his cereal, let me go. (*Frees hand, goes to kitchen.*) Go away and lock the door with your bent nail —better yet, leave it with the superintendent. My husband lost his key. ... (*To baby*) Good baby, going to get your cereal right away. (*Going in kitchen, sees hand still inside, gets big plastic spoon.*) Go away! Look, I'm losing my patience. ... Look, I'm going to punish you. ... Look, I'm going to stab you with this spoon and chop off all your fingers ... you don't believe me? (*Hits hand with spoon —boy screams—woman, frightened, looks at spoon then runs to window.*) Signora, I hit him with the spoon. ... What should I do, Signora? ... Take a patent out on it? What are you saying?! ... Disinfect him? Right, you're right, I need to disinfect him. ... Yes, I have it, my husband gives me everything. (*Takes alcohol from small table and runs to door.*) Stay still. ... No, it doesn't sting, it's the baby's. ... Darling, darling, what a wound I've given you, forgive me! There. Go away now. ... One kiss? (*Kisses hand*) On the mouth? No, on the mouth you will have nothing. ... No. I'm sorry, I will not take off the chain. ... I can't get my head through the crack, I have ears!! ... You're so persistent. (*Puts head in crack.*) Let me go ... let me ... my head! My head is stuck in the door! Push, push ... not with your mouth, foolish! With your hand! (*Gets head out with difficulty.*) Ahia, it hurts! My face is all scratched. (*Moves away from door. Boy knocks frantically.*) Stop it! (*Boy stops*) You think this is the time to play jazz in my house?! (*Boy tries to withdraw, but can't.*) Get out! ... What's the matter? ... What a disaster! (*Runs to window*) Oh, Signora, Signora ... his hand is stuck in the door! ... He's going to grow old with his arm in my house. ... My husband's going to kill me. What shall I do? ... Ah, yes, water with soap ... like for rings ... (*Toward peeping Tom's window.*) Go away. (*To neighbor*) Hot, hot will be better. ... (*To peeping Tom*) Lesbian. (*Running around stage*) Peep for peeping Tom, hot water for the boy, cereal for baby (*Honking*), a touch for the toucher ... (*Phone rings*) the heavy breather! (*Goes to phone*) Pronto, pig. (*Changes tone, thinks it's husband.*) Ciao ... What? Who is this? ... I'm sorry. I thought it was my husband. No, I didn't think it was my husband. No, my husband is not here. ... Would you care to leave a message. ... Yes, yes. ... (*Laughs to herself*) You know what I say to that? Congratulations. Let's hope it's a boy. Look, you have the wrong number. ... yes, a man lives here, my husband, but he gets only me pregnant! ... No? ... Your daughter. No, he didn't mention anything to me ... That pig! How old is your daughter? ... Sixteen. ... Ah, not quite sixteen, not bad ... I

mean. ... But, excuse me, listen to me, instead of letting
your sixteen-year-old daughter run around getting pregnant
by other people's husbands, lock her in the house. My husband locks me in the house, at my age, and you lock. ...
Bastard. (*Hangs up—to neighbor.*) He called me a whore! My
husband gets his daughter pregnant and he calls me a
whore! (*Boy knocks on door to get her attention.*) Don't bother me.
The family is disgraced. My husband's pregnant. (*Goes into
kitchen, comes out with basin and cereal. Exits bedroom.*) Here I
am, honey bunch ... stop it stupid. ... Don't pull me. ...
This cereal's boiling! (*Honk of horn*) Heaven help me! (*Enters*)
Signora, what am I going to do! ... The boiling cereal spilled
right in his eyes. ... No, not the baby, my brother-in-law. ...
What shall I do? (*Brings brother-in-law out, to neighbor.*)
Unguentine, certainly, I have Unguentine, yes, yes, I have
it, my husband gives me everything ... (*To boy who knocks.*)
Leave me alone. I've burned my brother-in-law. (*Takes
Unguentine from table, runs to wheelchair.*) Here I am, are you
burned? You should have been careful! I told you I had the
cereal in my hand. ... Stop it with that hand. (*He tries to hold
her down tight.*) Let me go, let me go. ... (*Tries to get free,
furious.*) I'll pour boiling water on you! (*He lets go*) Ah, at last
you catch on! (*Runs to boy*) Quick, put your hand in here. ...
No, it's not boiling. ... That was just to scare my brother-in-
law. (*Boy puts hand in ... screams—withdraws from crack.*) It was
boiling? Anyway, it worked, you got your hand out. No, go
away. ... You got burned? Here, put some Unguentine on
it. ... (*Passes it through door—boy pulls as far as she can go and tries
to have intercourse.*) What are you doing. ... Let me go. ... Are
you crazy? Let me go! Look, if someone sees us they'll take
us to jail with the door in the middle! Let me go! You make
me sick ... You have no respect for me ... Look, I'm going to
castigate you! Ah, you don't think so? Look! (*Slams door. Boy
screams and runs. Woman is desperate. Takes chain off door and
throws it open. Returns sadly to table and begins talking to neighbor.*)
I castigated him ... Because he tricked me ... I believed it
was really LOVE ... but no ... he's just like all the others ...
(*Desperate*) Signora, I can't go on any longer ... (*Baby cries*) I

can't go on any longer—my baby. ... I'm going to my baby.
... I'm happy with my baby ... (*Goes toward room, stops when phone rings. Brother-in-law starts honking.*) Be quiet, be quiet, stupid! Stop, stop! (*Baby cries, phone rings, brother-in-law honks louder—woman loses control.*) Enough! Enough! (*Takes gun, points it at throat.*) I'll kill myself, I'll kill myself ... (*Total silence a few seconds. Neighbor is talking to her. Woman looks at her.*) Yes ... yes. ... (*Holding back tears*) Yes! (*Puts down gun*) What was I doing ... God ... thank you, Signora. ... Why did you wait so many years before you came to live across from me. ... Yes, I'll do it now ... such a good idea ... (*Honking.*) Yes, dear, I'm coming, I'm here, all for you! Come on. (*Honking*) Come on! (*Pushes chair to front door.*) Let's go out for a little sexy walk! (*Pushes him out door. Great bump. Then a sequence of bumps and honks.*) Look out for the glass doors! (*Noise of shattering glass.*) That's one!! (*Baby cries. Woman goes toward bedroom; in middle of stage, stops. Looks at peeping Tom, smiles languidly, greets him ... slowly, sexily, glides to table, throwing kisses, gives him a "peek" of her shoulder. Quickly grabs gun and shoots.*) Peeping Tom peeps no more! (*Starts for baby, but phone rings. With a terrible voice.*) Pronto!! (*Changes tone*) Aldo! (*Almost sweet*) Yes, I've calmed down ... Yes, yes, everything's quiet here. ... Yes, you can come up ... I'm waiting for you. (*Leaves phone off hook. To neighbor.*) No, Signora, don't worry. (*Takes gun*) I'm calm ... I'm very calm. (*Points gun at door.*) I'm waiting ... very calmly.

BLACKOUT

MAMMA FRICCHETONA
(THE FREAK MOMMY)

MAMMA

Damn it, those pig cops ... even inside the church they come to arrest me. Now where do I hide? In the sacristy? Where is the sacristy? On this side or that side? (*Always trying to hide.*) There are the other two, damn it, they've cornered me ... the confessional ... I'll hide in the confessional. ... (*Tries to enter the confessional but it is locked.*) There's someone in there. It's a priest. They're everywhere, these damned priests! Well, I'll confess myself ... I want to see if the police have the guts to interrupt the sacred sacrament. (*She kneels on the right side of the confessional. Quietly.*) Hello ... uh, that is ... Father, Father! Cazzarola! He's fast asleep! (*Knocks with knuckles or fingers on the grate.*) Father, Father, wake up! It's about time. I would like to be confessed and if it is possible, in a hurry! It's not possible? You can't keep your eyes open? ... Ah, this I have never heard, a priest who before he hears confession wants to go for a cup of coffee! Oh no, you are not getting out of there or I'll make such a scene! ... It is my sacred right to be confessed ... I'm a taxpayer! ... What have taxes go to do with it? If I'm not mistaken we have a state religion and if I'm not mistaken your salary is paid by the State, namely me, taxpayer: Therefore I demand that my state religion confess me. You, Father, confess me. I am having such a burst of faith that I am going to explode. Let's go, Father, then when we're finished, I'll treat you to a coffee at the hot dog vendor outside ... shall we begin? ... We shall begin! ... What? The last time I confessed? Let me think a minute! ... Of course, I believe, otherwise would I be here confessing, how dare you! ... Twenty years ago ... the last time I confessed was exactly twenty years ago, my wedding day ... in church yes. What a beautiful ceremony! To tell the truth, I didn't want to get married in church ... but

I did it to please his mother, she really believes. ... No, no.
Father, I believe, but I'm also a Communist, a Communist
believer! ... Yes, okay, "One is not able to say that one has
been very faithful": Twenty years without confessing, I confess, is serious, very serious. ... But, here I am ... think of it
... twenty years later ... Communist and all. ... Shall we
start? Yes, I'm ready (*Stands up solemnly*) I swear to tell the
truth and nothing but ... (*Stops suddenly*) What am I doing?
Ah si, scusi, I made a mistake. ... Mi scusi, Father, but you
know, it's what you say down at the Palace of Justice (*Sits
relaxed on step of the confessional.*) ... Oeuhh, yes, yes, yes, there
are lots of times I've been to the Palace of Justice (*Takes out
work and starts knitting.*) ... aggravated assault on a public of-
ficial, accessory to robbery, not so hot as an accessory if they
collared me! More like an impediment—don't you think?
No, I'm not a chronic criminal, just every so often. ... Once
in a while, just to keep my spirits up.

Certainly I have a family: a husband and a son. ... No,
they don't steal. ... Yes, I live away from home. ... Well,
wherever: sometimes here, sometimes there ... I know, I
know, as wife and mother I am not this great model of virtue, but if I became this freak that I am it's precisely because
I was too too much that "model of virtue." I, to my son,
would give even my blood. I, to be close to my son, to be
able to bring him up, I myself quit even my job ... a job I liked.
... I was head of my section and also a union member. I
brought him up as if he were Jesus Christ. And I ... it seemed
to me I was the Virgin Mary ... and my husband ... St.
Joseph, the ox, and the ass all rolled into one! Then he grew
up, he went to school, and jumped right into the middle of this
dirty politics. ... Si, when he got to high school, you know, the
occupations, the fights with the police. One time he came home
all beaten up, covered with blood ... I swooned, terrified,
Father, I swooned! And from that day, all the times he was a
little late, or I heard the ambulance siren: "It's my son, it's
my son" I would scream. Father, Father, you don't know
what it is to be a mother, Father! Mother of a student
revolutionary!

And then at home my baby boy, he would fight about
everything with me and my husband ... you know, we are
obedient devoted militants of the Communist party. The
kindest words he could say to us: Revisionists, Social
Democrats, Opportunists, sell-outs of liberalism and
(*Screams*) "Where are you going now?" No, Father, not you,
we've only just met ... to my son I was saying it: "And
where are you going now?"

"Out with my comrades."

"Because we, I and your Father, are not comrades?"

"No, you are the family."

And he would taunt me with "family" as if he was
throwing a sack of sh——semolina at me. "No, no, it's you
who are not comrades," I would answer, "You are juvenile
delinquents, you are hoodlums ... cowards you are!"

"No, you are cowards who kiss the asses of the Chris-
tian-Democrats."

To me and my husband, get it, Father? "The Communist party has gone to Mass—it's kissing the Christian-
Democrats' Ass!" (*Repeat*) And off he'd go!

You know something, Father, that I got so desperate I
went to all those student riots! Oh, I couldn't do it, stay
home waiting for them to deposit him on my doorstep, beautiful but dead! I marched with the students, even ten steps
behind him, and I kept my eye on him without his seeing me
... the most awful thing was that to be inconspicuous I had to
shout the slogans they shouted and when they were shouting
about the Fascists it was okay but when I had to shout at the
top of my voice against the Communists, God, God ... I felt
so bad! And then, to march, to run (*Stands up and marches to
the other side of the confessional.*) and every time that ... (*Knocks
on grate*) Father, I'm here, Father. ... (*Sits*) No, I'm not
restless, that is how we marched at the demonstrations! And
every time I was shouting those slogans, ugh! I'd make eye
contact with someone from Party headquarters, once it was
the secretary, on the sidewalk saw me, heard me shout those
slogans, immediately crossed himself with the sign of the
hammer and sickle. And so they threw me out of the party,

all for love of my son! How it has betrayed me, love, Father! How it has betrayed me! Don't fall in love, believe me, Father ... you know, one time at the demonstration I was given advance information: "What's the demonstration tomorrow, Comrade?" "Peaceful." So I dressed for peaceful: shoes with heels so high (*Makes with hand the height.*), a skirt tight tight ... a police attack like you hadn't seen in a hundred years! ... They were all out after us: police, army, it seems to me the cavalry and the Pope's Swiss Guards! I had to run with those high heels ... if I'd fallen I'd have broken all the femurs I have ... to run faster I had to pull that skirt way up to here and all those police came after me! I shouted at them, "What do you want? Go away!" Mamma, what a race from Piazzale Loretto to Bovisa. ... I must have run fifty-four kilometers, all running! ... I felt so bad, all sweaty, my heart was coming out of me. ... I felt so bad ... my ovaries were hard-boiled. (*Priest reproaches her*) Oh, yes, "Don't talk like that, don't talk like that." I'd like to see you, Father, ever try to run in high heels. (*Resumes story telling*) Smoke everywhere! Tear gas, hand grenades, molotov cocktails ... and I had also lost my son and I called him: "Son, my son". ... All the sons of other mothers answered me ... at one point I see my son across the street, in the hands of a cop with his belt whip, whap across my son's little white face ... then I didn't see him anymore. I howled like a coyote. I flew across that street, never mind the tear gas bombs whizzing by at the level of a man's chest ... also a woman's! I grabbed the cop by his helmet and with my teeth attached myself to his ear. ... I would have eaten it up! I would have bitten it off if his pals hadn't come to pull me off. You shouldn't do that! But I'm telling you, Father, it is my son, you know! I made him—nine months to manufacture him ... I made all of him: two eyes, ten fingers, mouthful of teeth, and that cop was going to smash it all up in five minutes! Anyway, my son was able to escape, he was. ... Me, no, they beat me up and took me to jail. They gave me a trial to end all trials! ... Such a fuss they made about that ear, Father, ... and it wasn't such

a great ear. The judge with a terrible voice tells me: "You
have attacked the ear of the state!" What I went through!
And all for love of my son. How it has betrayed me, love,
Father ... my marriage, for example, was a marriage of love
(*Inspired*)—how I loved my husband, Father (*Changes tone*) ...
before we got married ... no, no even after ... but after we
set up housekeeping the shit—our ideological differences—
hit the fan. What? Yes, I did not agree with my husband's
ideological, social, moral, political, domestic behavior. And,
yes, because I was working, even I, eight hours a day like
him, with one substantial difference: That when we got
home I kept on working for another eighty ... wash, iron,
make the beds, cook ... he, no! He'd fall into the armchair
and click 6:15 TV for children, *HEIDI*!! "Oh, no, this isn't
fair: I work hard all day too—I told him—I'm just as tired as
you are. Who said the liberation of woman starts when she
gets a job and earn money? I got a money job but who's doing the housework? I'm still doing it! And who's paying me?
Nobody! Beautiful woman's liberation: With marriage I
landed two full-time jobs! On top of that my husband got
asthma, anxiety asthma, when I'd start cussing out the
saints, yes, well ... you understand me, Father ... I couldn't
take it anymore ... "I'm leaving you" I'd shout, he ...
"Plaff"—he'd have himself an attack—ah ahahahahah.
Dried up like a cod fish, he'd stop breathing—ahahahahah
—terror seized me, "Darling I won't leave you. I'll never
leave you, I'll always be here!" As soon as I quieted him
down, the attack was over and I was stuck again. Then it
turned out I was pregnant! ... But no, Father, I didn't think
it was a disgrace. ... I wanted this son ... it was part of my
five-year plan! I was happy to be pregnant ... how happy I
was! Nine months of puking! Always in bed for fear of losing
it and I said to myself in a burst of inspiration between
vomits, "This son is going to change my whole life—I'd tell
myself—what is a woman without children? Not a woman,
only a female!" What an asshole I was! Oh, sorry, Father, I
meant that shi. ... Well, you do it yourself, Father! Yes,
finally I get to my sins ... but you know, if I don't give you

the preamble, you would misunderstand! That's good,
okay, we'll skip everything and come to two years ago. I
discover that my son takes drugs! How do I know if they are
hard or soft ... for me, it is enough to hear the word "drugs"
to have a breakdown! He's depraved, he's antisocial, he's a
monster!—I would scream desperately—"Where did I go
wrong?" I would ask myself ... and to my husband! "Where
did you go wrong?" and he ahhha ... ahhaa ... (Repeat
asthma attack) And he and his little friends: "Take it easy,
heroin that kills is one thing, but a joint every so often!"
And I, pointing the finger of a conscientious mother, "It is
not okay! Drugs are an ideological choice, either stop taking
drugs or get out of my house, you, your street gang, and
your little whores!" And he: "What have you said! You've
offended my friends! I'm leaving home!" "Where," says I,
"to your grandmother?" "No, I'm leaving home!!"
      I, stone ... I didn't budge an inch.
      "Go, beautiful, don't think I care" ... —and my heart:
patapam, patapam—"I want to see how long you'll stay
away ... three days maximum, then you'll be back, to your
Mamma!" A week goes by, he doesn't come. I couldn't
sleep anymore, I couldn't eat anymore. And my husband
(Repeat asthma attack): "Ahaaa, ahaaa." I went looking for
him everywhere: in occupied schools, in the occupied build-
ings. ... No one would tell me anything! You get it, I was a
mother! Symbol of repression: Total silence: "These people
don't talk to me because I'm a mother? I'll show them ... I'll
disguise myself! ... As what? As a freak. Yes, freak, Father
... freaks? They are boys and girls who smoke a little ... steal
a little, they don't work. ... They live a good life, believe me!
I think I am a little old to be a freak. "I'll be a gypsy, a gypsy
has no age!" I said to myself. I went to one of those flea
markets where they sell used clothes, odd pieces, oriental
originals made in Monza, got myself decked out: Syrian
sandals, a skirt from Morocco, a jacket from Afghanistan, a
T-shirt U.S. Army issue, a Greek scarf from Woolworth's,
violet eyelids, tiny spot of red tin foil glued to my forehead,
my sister's gold tooth that fell out of her mouth when she

sneezed three years ago—I stuck it on my incisor here in
front—rings, glass beads, stuff on the ears. I went to a com-
mune of assorted male and female freaks with a few vagrants
thrown in, I go in (*Parades to other side of confessional.*). I look
like a Christmas tree! Shaking all over! (*Knocks on grate.*) I'm
here, Father ... but pay more attention! So, I go in ... not
even the dog, I say the dog never noticed me. I go in and sit
on my little mat, and put down my stuff, get ready to go to
sleep. At just the right moment I take out a little bottle of this
stuff I had made: essence of turpentine, oil of the liver of
cod, excrement of horse, strong tobacco, pure alcohol, tinc-
ture of iodine, a little toothpaste for color ... creosote for
outhouses, some drops of lemon that never spoils. I put it to
my nose and sniff sniff sniff lost in drugged ecstacy. After
three seconds all the male and female freaks are sitting
around me. "What are you doing?" "I'm turning on."
"What is it?" "Hard stuff!!" "Will you give us a hit?"
"Hey, watch out, I don't want to kill anyone." And they
would sniff my little bottle up their noses almost all the way
up to their brains and say "Mamma, what a drug!!" It was
the toothpaste ... it went to your head!! Poor kids, how easily
they're taken in. "Who are you? Where did you come
from?" I was suddenly so interesting. The story I told,
Father! My mother was from India ... my father, gypsy
from Calabria. I live casting spells and reading cards and the
stars. I feed on only hen's blood and blood of freshly killed
cats because I'm a witch. No, they didn't believe me but
they liked me and let me stay with them. ... (*Pause*) My son?
Never saw him! Only once, far from me, at the concert at
the stadium. "Damn it, now I'll get him." I said to myself. I
start for him, at that moment the riot breaks out! They
charge! Set fire to the speakers, the stage, the singer, the
police arrive ... guess who they arrest first. Bravo! When they
put the cuffs on me I said, "Good evening I've been worried
about you." They locked me up but right away they let me
out ... after three days because I didn't have any accessories
to the combustibilities on me. I come out of jail and see this
mob of people, freaks, metropolitan Indians, feminists, they

were waiting for me! They're yelling, singing ... they hug
me ... they've made a big banner with the words "FREE
MAMMA WITCH." It was a celebration if I do say so, a
mob scene. I didn't know I had so many friends. I hadn't
done anything for them they just loved me for me. In front of
everybody a girl comes up holding a live chicken: "Here's a
hot cappucino for you," she says. And so I began to hang
around with those boys and girls, listening to what they were
saying. First I didn't understand anything, then I got it. They
were saying, "What is personal is political! You need to confront your sexuality!" ... Yes, sexuality, Father. Grab hold of
life, enjoyment, use you imagination! Refuse the ideology of
work. (*Gregorian chant*) "Work makes man free, it was written
on the wall of a beer hall, of a German beer hall!" No? You
don't like Gregorian chant? Yes, Father, I'll behave myself.
(*On knees*) Yes, Father, I'm listening. (*Repeats after him*) I have
fallen into the abyss, the infernal abyss ... moral disorder ...
we must have order mustn't we, Father, order, rules, regula-
tions, rules to live by, rules of the game, rules of etiquette, the
little girl needs her book of rules! All my life, from when I was
born, I hear repeated these rigmaroles!

(*Stands up, faces audience authoritatively.*)

Hop, hop, get in line, go to bed.
Pay attention, behave, quiet!
Hop, hop, on your feet, sit down, wash up.
Button up, get in line two at a time.
Mm-mm, eat your cereal, sck, sck, take the nipple,
Grunt, grunt, make the poopoo! Stay!
Beddy-bye. Mamma is pretty, Daddy is good
In line, little boys over here
Little girls over there.
Little boys make wee-wee standing up
Little girls make it sitting down.
The potty for the poopoo: Everybody sit down.
Poopoo is the same for everyone!!
Don't touch poopoo,
Don't play with poopoo!

Poopoo is cacca! Take your little hand off the cacca!

(*Speaking to imaginary little boy on her left.*) Take your little
hands off your pipi! Don't touch pipi! Don't play with pipi.
(*With caressing voice*) Pisellino ... (*Turns to imaginary little girl on
her right, severe.*) Passerina!!

Little boys don't touch pipi because pipi is cacca!
Little boys don't touch little girls,
Because little girls are cacca and poopoo!

If that is so, you know what I tell you, Father? Listen
carefully to me because I don't want to be misunderstood, I
have found out one thing: Love is messy! Life, liberty,
dreams, are messy! In respect to the order you want to give
us, Father: Make love without so much superstructure,
engagement, dowry, marriage. "I want you to meet my
parents." ... To make love for love so beautiful! ... I tell you
it is the most beautiful ... try it once! I, Father, made love to
a boy whose name I can't even remember anymore ... but I
remember his eyes his nose his mouth and his words. I
remember his hands and the things he told me while we
making love! "God! Holy Mother! Jesus Christ! It is so
good. I think I'm in heaven!" And he was an atheist! ...
Was I lost? And if I tell you that I was found? To be free, it's
the greatest! Nobody's going to make me go back to my
family, I told my son that ... (*Pause*) Yes he came to look for
me, he found me right away ... He was well dressed, in a
suit, with his hair cut, a necktie, "I came home, Mother, I
got tired of life as a bum, I got it together, I don't smoke,
I've got a job, I got bored with politics and Poppa's doing
great, too, he's playing tennis, he doesn't have any more
asthma attacks, he's got a girl but if you'll come home he's
giving her up immediately. "COME HOME MAMMA"
(*Mimics vomiting*) I felt sick! Yes, because I had, like a flash,
me back there, in my house, with all the aggravations, the
shopping, the shirts to iron, without ever a minute for
myself. You know, Father, if I wanted to read the newspaper, the toilet!! If one day my intestines didn't function,

I lost out on the latest news! "No, my son, I don't think so.
... I'm not ready yet ... you should understand. ..." But
aren't you ashamed? You go around like a bum!". ... "Yes,
you're right, but I won't be a bum. I'll find a job, a little
one, part time, to make enough to eat and sleep, the rest of
my time I want to spend with people, with women ... to give
what I have inside. How full I am of beautiful things ... to
take what people have to give me ... to have experiences ... I
want to talk, laugh, sing. I want to be able to look at the sky.
... Do you know, my son, that the sky is blue and I didn't
know that anymore? No, my darling, I can't go home, not
even if you send the police to take me. ... And they, in fact,
did send the police to take me! Exactly. My son and my husband got out a warrant against me for abandoning the con-
jugal bed. Imagine, Father, the cops have had the guts to
follow me even into the church ... Where are they? There,
by the sacristy. You don't see them? ... Father, what are you
doing? Father, don't call them ... are you crazy? What
about the sanctity of the confessional ... (*Runs to grab her bag.*)
You can't do a thing like this to me ... stop it!!! (*Runs toward
exit*) No, I don't want to go home with the police ... (*Caught
and handcuffed*) Okay. Let's go. I'm over twenty-one! I will
decide my own fate. (*Stops suddenly and yells to confessional.*)
You squealed, you squealed, you're no son of Mary! You
squealed. You're no son of Mary!

BLACKOUT

WAKING UP

(One-room apartment. MAN *and* WOMAN *in bed, asleep. Baby in bassinet.)*

WOMAN

Three pieces, one weld, "Hit the compressor!" ... Two bolts, one weld, "Hit the slicer!" ... *(Howl)* My God! I've cut off all my fingers! My fingers. ... Help me pick them up ... the boss doesn't like. ... They make a mess. *(Wakes up)* My fingers! I won't be able to pick my nose!! *(Looks at hand)* They're here ... I was dreaming! Shit, now I'm dreaming about that job, isn't it enough all day at the factory? What time is it? *(Looks at clock)* Half past six? *(Gets up, puts on robe and slippers.)* It didn't go off, the bastard! Mamma mia am I late! *(Runs to cradle, picks up baby.)* Let's go, baby, let's go! *Sings:* "Daybreak, another new day!" Wake up, wake up, Mama's little sweetheart, hurry up! *(Puts baby on table to change it.)* Pee pee, you pee peed again. I just changed you at three o'clock this morning. Pissy, pissy pisspot and I'm so late. We'll have to run all the way to the nursery, if we don't get there by seven the nun sends us right back home. *(Undresses baby)* Now mommy's going to wash your little bottom. *(Turns on hot water.)* Hot water? No, there is no hot water ... I bet that idiot Luigi turned off the boiler last night. No, he's not an idiot, here's the hot water. *(Takes baby to sink.)* Let's wash baby's face. *(Starts talking loudly, then remembers* MAN *is asleep.)* Shshshsh, don't cry, you'll wake up Daddy. Lucky Daddy can sleep another half hour ... and then he's flying like Superman to the factory, ahhh fly to the bus, fly to the train, and then at the factory. *(Puts baby on table to wipe him with dish towel.)* Bompbomp blimp boom bompbomp blimp boom, trained monkey on the assembly line, bompbomp blimp boom. ... Ah, ah, baby's laughing. ... You like to see mommy acting like a trained monkey ... Now you're done, now a nice little sprinkle of ... *(Mistake, stunned)* grated cheese. ... Who put the grated cheese in the talcum powder.

... Mamma mia, what a mess. ... Wait, I'm going to save it,
it's to expensive to waste. ... Your bottom was perfectly
clean. ... (*Dressing baby frantically*) Quickly, quickly, little
pissypot! Here we go! All ready! What time is it? God, I'm
so late. Stay still a minute while mommy takes a quick
washy, washy. (*Washes hands and face.*) Camay, soap of the
stars, Camay, soap ... water, there's no more water, damn
it! A family like this in a building like this with three hundred other families like this all with faces to wash at the same
hour!! What am I going to rinse this off with now! It's not
fair! That Camay stings my eyes! (*Wipe with dish towel.*) I'll
wash later. Who looks at me anymore, anyway ... nobody
... (*Brushes hair*) ... but they sure do smell me ... I'll put on
some deodorant ... (*Spray can*) What a wonderful invention,
spray! Let's spray ourselves a little, it will hide mommy's
smell ... ouch, that burns. ... What is this? (*Reads can*) ...
Silver radiator paint ... I've got a silver armpit? How'm I
going to get it off. ... I'll get it off with solvent at the factory.
(*Pulls on her clothes ... wraps baby in blanket ... runs to door.*)
Ready! Set! Go! Quarter of seven. ... We're going to make
it! Take mommy's pocketbook, mommy's jacket. (*Starts for
door, stops suddenly.*) The key, the key, where did I put the
key, every morning the saga of the key! I have to spend my
time trying. ... (*Rummages in pockets*) Don't get hysterical!!
Don't get hysterical!! ... Try to remember everything that I
did last night. So, I came home, Luigi wasn't here ... I
opened the door, baby under mommy's right arm, pocketbook under mommy's left arm, and key in left hand. ... Put
pocketbook here, the baby I put in the crib. ... Went back
out, got grocery bag, key still in hand, milk bottle under left
arm, came back in. ... Put the bag down here, the milk I put
in the fridge ... I bet I put the key in the fridge, too. (*Opens
fridge door*) No, not there ... not in the egg tray, not in the
butter dish. I didn't put in the milk either, but I put in the
lemon-flavored laundry detergent. It's okay, okay, lemons
are always kept in the fridge or they go bad! ... I am crazy, I
am crazy. ... The milk I put in the washing machine. ... Not
there. ... Lucky. ... Where did I put the milk? On the stove,

so I could heat it up for baby, that's it, and I needed both hands to open the milk bottle. ... I put the key between my teeth. ... I'll never know why I put it between my teeth and not on the table. ... Then I light the stove, *so*, the milk for the baby is on the stove, I've lit the baby, I mean I've lit the milk, I've lit the gas! ... I leave the milk to boil and go to undress the baby. (*Goes to crib, miming action.*) I take the baby, I put him on the table. ... No, with the baby in my arms I go to the closet to get the tub for the baby's bath ... the key still between my teeth. ... I put the tub on the table, I look for the baby. ... There's no baby. ... I've lost my baby. Where did I put the baby? (*Runs to furniture she names.*) In the fridge, in the washing machine, in the closet. ... I put the baby in the closet! Lucky he started to cry or I never would have found him! My poor little baby. ... I was so upset I had to get a glass of water. (*Stops, gulps*) What do you bet I swallowed the key? Of course, because I still had it between my teeth. ... No, I couldn't have swallowed it ... my key has a hole in it, I would have whistled all night, and what a scene Luigi would have made about that. Where did I put the key? Don't get hysterical! I take the tub, I go to fill it with hot water, I take the bicarbonate (*Takes a jar*) because I always put two spoonfuls in baby's bath ... maybe it fell out of my teeth. (*Looks in bicarb*) Sugar!! Who put sugar in the bicarbonate (*Looks in other box.*) and bicarbonate in the sugar? Ah-ha, that's why the sister at the nursery said, "I have to keep your baby in the school, when I put him in the yard bees and wasps swarm all over him." Poor baby! And Luigi, the scene he made over the coffee. ... I had put in the bicarb! The burps he made! And the key, where did I put the key?! But let's see. No, wrong, all wrong. ... I didn't take the key out of the keyhole yesterday, oh yessss, because when I was giving the baby his bath I heard Luigi raving outside the door because I left my key in the keyhole. I took the key out of the door, he came in ... yelling like crazy, I had the key in my hand, I'm sure of that ... I shook it in his face. I wanted to poke his eyes out. I said, "I forgot the key in the lock, so what, kill me, wife killer!" "Leave me alone," he says to me, "I'm not

mad because of the key ... the fuckin' train was an hour late
... an hour and a half to go twelve miles ... does the boss pay
me for that? No he doesn't pay me to get to work, or get
home, or the bus. All those trips I make for the boss, free for
nothing!'' ''And you come home and get mad at me?'' I said
that still with the key in my hand. "Anyway, the boss is not
called boss anymore, he's called Multinational Corporation.
The Multinational Corporation steals your travel money
and you get mad ... you don't get mad about what he steals
from me, work 8 hours like a slave for him and then come
home to be your free maid. For him, for the Multinational
Corporation!'' At that moment I was giving the baby his
bottle. (*Goes to crib*) I took him in my arms ... it might have
fallen in here. ... That does it, that does it, that does it, one
more time! Poopoo, poopoo, pooper! How many time do I
have to tell you to do your poopoo at the nursery. ... At two
minutes past seven you should do it so the nun can change
you. ... What time is it? ... Oh God, so late. ... I won't
make it, I won't make it. ... I lose the day ...? Look what ...
I don't understand how with such a tiny bottom you make a
poopoo so big!! (*Washes baby again*) The family, this sacred
family; they have invented it on purpose so that all you guys
who get your balls cut off every day at those degrading jobs
can come home and take it out on us wives, us mothers, us
home makers! Mattresses for you to punch out. (*Finishes
washing baby, etc.*) We put you together again, for the
Multinational Corporation! Free of charge! To be ready the
next morning, handsome and raring to go to produce more
for him, Mr. Multinational Corporation; he is everbody's
daddy! Luigi starts to laugh, "Hey, here I have a feminist
wife and I didn't know it. ... How long have you been going
to feminist meetings?'' ''Listen, stupid,'' I told him, ''I
don't need to hang around with feminists to know our life is
shit. We work like two dogs, we never have a minute to say
two words, to be together. Do you ever ask me, ''Are you
tired?'' ''Can I help?'' Who does the cooking? Me. Who
does the dishes? Me. Who does the shopping? Me. Who
does the somersaults to get to the end of the month ... Me,

me, me! And I have a job, too! The socks you get dirty. Who
washes them? Me. How many times have you washed my
socks? Is this marriage? I want to be able to talk to you, I
want to live with you, not just exist! You never think that I
might have some problems. It's okay with me that your problems are mine but I wish also that my problems would be
yours and not always only yours mine and mine always
mine!! I want to be able to talk, talk with you, but when you
get home from work you conk out! Then, every night, TELE-
VISION. Every Sunday, SOCCER. You watch 22 idiots in
their underpants kicking a ball around, with another mentally
defective maniac also in his underpants but with a striped
shirt and a whistle. He, Luigi, purple, you'd think I said
something bad about his mother. ... He says to me, "But,
what, you want to learn about sports now?" That was not exactly the right answer! I screamed like a maniac, let him have
it. I couldn't help it! I got nasty, he got nastier, I got nastier,
then he got nastier. Finally I said, "If this is marriage, I wish
to say I've made a mistake." I picked up my mistake (*Picks up
baby and heads for door.*) and started to leave. At that point, the
key, I had it in my hand. ... I'm sure because I unlocked the
door, Luigi got up, his face, poor Luigi, was white like a
sheet, poor guy. I'd never made a scene like that before. He
held on to me, "Don't go like that, listen." "Let me go."
"Let's talk, first let's talk, and then if you want to go, go, but
first let's talk. Let's discuss it, okay?" So he leads me to the
(*Indicates bed*) discussion, sits me down, and tells me that yes,
I'm right that he was used to being babied by his mother, that
he thought he could treat me like his mama, he was wrong, he
needed to change, it was so tender the way he was saying it
that I started crying, the more he blamed himself the more I
cried, the more I cried the more he blamed himself, it was so
beautiful to cry like that last night ... and the key ... sure he
took it, he put it in the pocket of his jacket. (*She sees his jacket
and looks in the pockets.*) Here it is, my key and his key. What
time is it? ... Ten to seven, we can still make it. ... Come on,
honey bunch, we're going to make it. Mommy's baby, mommy's jacket, mommy's pocketbook. (*Stops dead at door.*) My

bus pass (*Puts baby on table.*), wait, let me look for the bus
pass 'cause if the bus is crowded I have to put you down to
look for it and someone will step on you. ... (*Looks in bag*)
Here it is. ... Six punches? Six going, six coming. ... Six going and six coming! Who made all these holes in the bus
pass? Six holes! ... What day is today? (*Looks at calendar on
wall. ... disturbed, discouraged, picks up baby almost without a
voice.*) Sunday? SUNDAY. (*Shouting—to baby*) And you
never told me. It's Sunday. I'm nuts. I wanted to go to work
on Sunday. I'm crazy. ... It's Sunday. (*Singing*) "Sunday is
not a working day. Sunday is a sleeping day." Back to bed,
baby, back to bed, sleep! (*Puts baby on bed and faces front.*) I
want to dream of a world where every day is Sunday. A
whole lifetime of Sundays. The end of the world. A burst of
eternal Sundays! No more weekdays, they hanged Monday,
shot Thursday, sliced up Friday! Every day is Sunday.
Sleep, baby, if I dream I am at work again I will personally
kill myself! Sleep! (*On the last words she pulls the sheet over her
head.*)

BLACKOUT

WE ALL HAVE THE SAME STORY

(In the center of an empty stage a platform on which lies a GIRL. *Lights are dim.)*

GIRL

No, no, please ... please ... stay still ... stop it. I can't breathe. Wait. ... Yes. I like to make love but I'd like ... well, a little more, what can I say? You're squashing me! Get off ... stop it! You're slobbering all over my face. ... No, not in my ear, no! Yes, I like it but your tongue feels like an egg beater! How many hands have you got? Let me breathe. Get off, I said! *(Sits up slowly, as if freeing herself from under a man, sits facing audience.)* Finally. ... I'm all sweaty. You think that's the way to make love? ... Yes, I love to make love, but I'd like it even more with a little love in it. ... How can you call me sentimental? I knew it. You couldn't wait to tell me I'm a romantic fool. ... Of course I want to make love, but I would like you to understand I'm not a pinball machine. You can't just put your money in the slot and expect all my lights to light up and ting bop-ckkk-ckkk-ckkk-bong-gong, gunk, gunk and you get as rough as you want. I'm not a pinball machine. You get rough with me, I go into tilt, get it? *(Gets up; talks to audience.)* ... Is it possible that if one of us doesn't lie down flat on her back, skirts up, pants down, legs flying and ready to go, she is a "repressed bitch with a Puritanical attitude inculcated by a reactionary-imperialist-capitalist, Catholic, conformist education?" ... I'm being a smart-ass, eh? Smart women bust your balls, right? ... Better to have a dumb blonde who wiggles and giggles. ... Why are you pinching me? ... No, it doesn't turn me off. ... Come on, let's do it, let's make love! *(Stretches out)* Ohh, you can be so sweet when you want to be, almost human! A comrade! With you I say things I never even think of with anyone else ... even smart things ... yes, you make me feel smart. With you I can be me ... and you're not going with me just to make love, you stay with me after we've done it ...

and I talk and you listen to me, you talk and I listen to you ...
you talk, you talk, and I ... and I ... and I. ... (*Reaching
orgasm, voice more and more languid; abrupt change in tone, realistic
and terrified.*) Please, stop. ... I'll get pregnant?!! (*Imploring*)
Stop a minute. (Peremptory) Stop!! (*He stops finally*) I have to
tell you something important. ... I'm not on the pill. ... Not
any more. ... It was making me sick, it was making my
breasts as big as the dome at St. Peter's. ... Yes, okay, we can
do it ... but please, pay attention. ... Don't forget what happened that other time. ... Oh, God it was awful. (*Changes tone*)
Yes, I know you felt awful, but I felt worse, okay! ... Yes, but
be careful. (*They start to make love again, she's rigid, starts tapping
foot or fingers nervously, looks at imaginary partner and says apprehen-
sively.*) Oh, careful. ... (*Upset*) I can't relax, the thought of getting pregnant makes my blood run cold!! ... Diaphragm?
Yes, I've got one, but you didn't tell me were going to do it
today ... anyway, I don't like that rubber thing in my belly.
... It's like chewing gum inside me. ... (*Man gets up, they sit
unhappy, facing audience.*) You've lost your enthusiasm? Well,
I'm sorry. ... It's funny if you think of it. I don't want to get
pregnant and you lose your enthusiasm. (*Angrier*) And you're
supposed to be a "comrade"? You make me laugh. ... You
know whose comrade you are? Your prick's! Oh, yes! That's
what does your thinking. It's him, your comrade! That's the
Catholic-imperialist-elitist-Puritan. Look, it has a cardinal's
cap on its head. With stripes like a general and it's making the
Fascist salute!! Yes, Fascist!! (*Indignant*) Bastard! (*Starts to cry*)
How could you say that to me? ... (*Crying*) I don't think with
my uterus. ... Yes, I'm crying, but you hurt me, you did!
(*Lies down abruptly, as if man pushed her.*) What? I cry and you
get excited? But, but ... yes ... yes. ... (*Full of love*) I do, I do, I
want to. Yes, I know it's not your fault. ... It's society's fault,
the egotism, the frustration, (*More languid*) the imperialism,
the multinational. ... (*Changes tone*) What's going on? Stop ...
stop. ... (*Goes limp. Flat voice.*) You didn't stop. (*Desperate*) I'm
pregnant. (*Jumps up*) I'm pregnant. ... (*Shouting*) I'm pregnant. ... (*Change of lights from low to bright. She's in M.D.'s office,
talking to a nurse.*) Yes, nurse, I'm pregnant. ... Three months.

... Yes, nurse, I've had the tests. ... Yes, nurse, I'll lie down
(*Does so*) ... please be gentle. ... Yes, I know it's only an ex-
amination and it doesn't hurt, but I'm nervous ... I've
already had one abortion ... with no anesthetic, no local, no
general. As they say, "Wide awake the whole time." ... It
was horrible ... the pain. But the worse thing was the way
they treated me ... as if I was a little whore. They wouldn't
let me scream. "Shut up," they said, "You made a mistake,
pay!!" (*Change tone*) And did I pay ... this time I want my
abortion done right ... I don't want any pain. I want to be
put to sleep. I don't want to feel anything ... I don't want to
know anything ... I don't even want to know when he does
it—put me to sleep a week ahead of time, then when he feels
like doing it, when he has time. ... (*Changes tone. Serious.*) A
million lire? One million!? Everything's going up, eh!? ...
Yes, yes, I understand—the anesthetist, the risk. ... (*Changes
tone*) A million lire? ... I know, nurse, I could get a legal
abortion. That's right, statue 194 ... I went berserk trying to
find a doctor who would write me a certificate or a hospital
to put me on the list. ... Finally I got called; I went in;
everyone objected to abortion! One doctor did them all ...
dead tired ... everyone else objected ... the nurses objected,
the ladies' auxiliary, the cook. ... The objections the cook
had. If it hadn't been for some girls who came to stage a pro-
abortion sit-in, we all would have starved to death. Then the
police arrived—they threw the girls out. ... I got scared. I
said to myself, "With the help of this statute 194, I am going to give birth to a 24-year-old son who has done his
military service, is unemployed, and all ready to emigrate to
America." I'll take my chances outside the law! (*Changes
tone*) A million lire. Now I understand why the gynecologists
object. ... It's a million lire for each objection. ... They'll all
become millionaires on our bodies.(*Rises decisively*) No,
nurse, I'm not doing it. ... No. It's not the money, I could
borrow. ... It's blackmail. ... There's a law. You respect it.
(*Changes tone, reflective*) I'll have it ... I'll have it. ... (*Half to
herself*) You have to have a child sometime. ... (*Finally decided*)
I'll be fulfilled. Yes, I'll be fulfilled!!! (*Shouting happily, jumps*

on to platform, back to audience marching, militant.) ...
Motherhood, motherhood!! Third month, fourth month,
fifth month. (*Turns to face audience.*) The breasts are swelling
up, the belly's swelling up. ... Prenatal exercises for a
healthy birth! One, two, three, four, flex. Pant like a dog,
aha, aha, aha, aha. ... Stretch: one, two, three, four. Pant
like a dog, aha, aha, aha, faster, my head is spinning ... I'm
going to faint. ... Oh, I'm going to throw up. ... Oooh, it's
moving! The baby's moving! Like wings fluttering! That's
so sweet, so sweet. (*Changes tone*) Ice cream ... ice cream ... I
want ice cream with whipped cream and pickles and spa-
ghetti! (*Professional tone*) Sharp sound from the abdomen
—aah, louder—aah ... louder—aah. ... It's starting, it's
starting. ... Yes, nurse, I'm lying down. ... Yes, nurse, I'm
relaxing. ... Yes, nurse, I'm panting like a dog ... ah, ah,
yes, I'm pushing ... oh, God, it hurts, it hurts, ahia—ahi, I
can't stand it anymore ... do something ... ahia ... ahia. ...
Where is he? Where is he? ... Outside? Doing what?
(*Changes tone*) Smoking nervously. (*To audience*) Poor thing.
... He's nervous ... and tense. ... Why couldn't he have
been more nervous in the beginning when he got me pregnant? (*Speaks to women in audience1.*) I don't know about you
but it really gets to me that with getting pregnant, it's the
woman "always" and the man "never!" I object. It's an
obsession with me. ... I even dream about it at night: I
dreamed that my boyfriend had breasts. Beautiful! Big!
Round!! I wanted to caress them a little and he said, "Leave
me alone." What do you think he thought he had there?!!
He explained to me that he was a she man, that's a special
kind of man ... who, if he has sexual intercourse with a
woman and hasn't used a contraceptive, he gets pregnant!
(*Touches his breasts*) You are so beautiful ... come on, lie
down. (*Lies down as if man is under her.*) Take your clothes off,
I want to talk to you. ... What is it? ... You seem nervous ...
tense. ... You're not on the pill? Forget it! I love you
anyway! Relax, baby, I'll take care of you ... doesn't matter
if you're not on the pill ... if you get pregnant there's this
statute 194 that takes care of you—if you want you can have

an illegal abortion, general anesthetic, I'll pay everything.
... If you decide you want to have the baby, I'll marry you.
(*Pressuring him*) Come on, let's make love, let's make love.
Forget about getting pregnant; a man is only fulfilled if he
becomes a mother! Mooootheruum. (*Gets in giving birth position.*) It's born! It's born! (*Sits looking left, full of hope.*) Is it a
boy?? ... (*Disturbed*) No? ... (*Dismayed*) What is it? (*As the
midwife, mimes everything*) Smack baby's bottom; smack
smack. Cry, wah, wah. Cut the umbilical cord; cckr. Tie the
knot. Put the baby in hot water; sciac. ... Cold; woof woof.
(*Turns to mother, baby on knee.*) My beautiful baby, brava,
brava! ... Feeding, Injection. Vaccination ... another injection. Enema. Yucck! What a beautiful poo-poo! Vomit!
Feeding. (*Mimes swallowing or sucking.*) Formula homogeniz-
ed, vitamins. Beautiful baby, funny, funny. No, don't cry.
Make a little burp. Play with your toys. ... Oh, how pretty
they are zooba, zooba, zooba! No, can't throw them on the
floor, play, the cereal, nò, don't spit it out. No, don't throw
the spoon on the floor. Aaaha, yum yum, good cereal. Don't
throw up. Naughty girl! Grow up! Grow up! Mama's
beautiful baby! Sit here (*Puts baby on her left.*) so I can tell you
a beautiful story. ... (*Through the story she moves and changes
voices as suits the characters.*) Now, once upon a time there was
a pretty little girl with a beautiful doll. The truth is, the doll
wasn't beautiful, she was all dirty, her hair was torn out and
she was made of rags, but the little girl loved her so much.
She talked to the doll and her doll answered her. Yes, it's
true, the dolly could say words but she only said dirty words
and the little girl learned and repeated them. "Where did
you learn such disgusting words," asked the little girl's
mamma. "My dolly," answered the pretty little girl!
"You're lying, dolls don't say bad words! Boys have taught
you!" "No, my dolly ... Dolly, say some words to Mama!"
The dolly who did everything the little girl told her because
she loved the little girl so much spit out a stream of dirty
words: "Bitch, fuck, shit (*Chanting*), asshole, asshole,
asshole!" Ohh!! Mama got all red in the face, grabbed the
doll from the little girl's hands, threw her out the window,

and plop—she landed in the backyard on the compost heap. "Wicked Mama! Wicked Mama!" said the little girl, running out into the backyard, but at that precise moment a giant red cat passing by grabbed the dolly in his teeth and went off into the woods. Crying and crying the little girl went after the cat. She searched and searched and walked and walked. ... She got lost in the woods. It got dark. ... The woods became a huge forest. Then, far off in the distance the little girl saw a tiny, tiny light. ... She walked toward the tiny tiny light. ... What was it? A dwarf, tiny, standing on top of a giant toadstool peeing phosphorescent pee pee! "Dwarf, little dwarf, have you seen a huge red cat with a rag dolly that says bad words in his mouth?" "There he is," and the dwarf squirts a huge stream of pee pee onto the cat and bripp-roo the huge red cat falls to the earth dead! Well, everyone knows, dwarf's pee pee is terribly poisonous to cats! "Thank you, thank you," squeals the little girl, hugging her dolly who is all soaked with pee pee. "Who is that fucking shit," screams the rag doll, "That asshole killed my big red cat that I love so much. He beat me up, he used me for a doormat, he ran right over me, made me work my ass off, did terrible things to me, but I loved him just the same. He used me like a slave, I cried, he made me sick, but I loved him even more because after all he made me feel like a woman, and not only that I had my very own MAN! Now, I don't have my big red cat, oh, you fuck of a dwarf, bastard, made of shit, what do I do?" "Oh, I love this dirty mouthed dolly," screeched the dwarf, "Oh, I love her! Maybe, maybe, I'll marry her!" "No, I'm going to marry her!" comes a terrible voice from the dark forest, no longer lit up with the dwarf's phosphorescent pee pee. ... Who is it? Oh, how scary!! A great big huge wolf, with great big long teeth! "I'm going to marry her!" "No, I don't want him," says the doll, "I don't want him, that busted ass of a wolf there." "I am not a busted ass of a wolf! I'm a computer programmer, a wicked witch turned me into a wolf ... the proof is I still have my software in my pocket ... if this little virgin will kiss me on the forehead I will immediately become a young man, with a profession, good looking, with graduate degrees, offering a relationship of love and affection.'' The little girl kissed the wolf ... and out jumped an unbelievably handsome computer programmer ... who was so happy he let out a huge fart right in the face of the dwarf, who dropped on the ground dead. Well, everyone knows, computer programmers' farts are very poisonous to dwarfs. When she saw the computer programmer the little girl fell madly in love. ''Oh, he's so handsome, he's so handsome!'' And the computer programmer, since time had gone by and the little girl had grown up ... and she had those round things that women have in front ... and also in back ... and computer programmers are so crazy for those round things ... it's, as a matter of fact, a course that they take in college. ... ''I've changed my mind,'' he says. ''I'm not going to marry the dolly, I'll marry the little girl with the bouncy tits and the round little bottom!'' So they got married and lived happily ever after! The day after, the little dolly says, ''Conference! Conference! Dear shitty married couple. Enough of this happy ever after. I here am all torn up to see you living this everyday chicken shit, oh, oh, oh, oh, oh, oh, life of yours and leaving me out. He goes off to his computers, and the little bride with your round bottom stays home moaning and groaning until night time and he comes home. ... He throws you on the bed and it's ah oh oh, ah oh oh ... and then in the morning you set the alarm clock and it's oh ah oh oh ... and then after lunch, which is very bad for your health, oh ah oh oh oh. ...'' ''But I am so happy,'' says the little grown-up girl who already had a little swelling up belly, ''I'm so in love!'' ''Don't give me that shit, 'I'm so happy,''' answered the rag doll. ''Balls, I've never seen a more pathetic twat in my life than you. A pathetic twat like me when I was living with my bad red cat ... but with him good, or bad, if you wanted to, you could fight things out politically, but with this computer programmer what can you do? So he doesn't beat you up, but he leaves you alone all day like a stupid shit ... he never says one word to you even, oh you fucking dummy!'' ''Listen, you revolting rag dolly,'' intones the computer programmer, young, good-looking, with graduate degrees, offering a relationship of love and affection, "Stop getting my wife excited or I'll flush you down the toilet." "Bravo," answered the vulgar dolly, "You go to the toilet, take a crap." To a computer programmer! "Right, I will go to the toilet and I'll take you with me and use you for toilet paper!" Having said that, the computer programmer grabs the rag dolly and goes into the bathroom and shut the door. "No. No, please don't do it, my husband, don't do a thing like that to my dolly. ... Open the door!" "No, I won't open the door. I'm here with my pants down and now I'm going to wipe myself!!" That very moment there's a terrible scream from the computer programmer, "Ahhhhhh." A computerized scream. ... What happened? When he wiped himself with the dolly. ... Woosh! She shot right up his bottom ... only her feet were sticking out. "Help me, my wife, it's disgraceful! This despicable dolly has shot up my bottom ... pull her out!" "I'm pulling, I'm pulling, but she doesn't come out!" "Help, it hurts, I'm going to die ... I'm going to give birth. Help! ... Go get the midwife!" The wife ran out to call the midwife. As soon as she opens the door of the house ... the ways of the Lord, as everyone knows, are infinite ... a midwife is passing the house ... with MIDWIFE written on her bosom ... backwards like AMBULANCE on a vehicle. "Oh, Signora midwife, Signora midwife, heaven has sent you. Please come in. ... We have a family problem." When the midwife found herself face to face with the bottom of the computer programmer, she says, "Isn't that sweet. You've put booties on him already. Is this man your husband?" "Yes." "Difficult delivery, feet first." And then she began to laugh ... I mean laugh ... and like all us women ... (*To the audience*) even you ... you know what happens when we get a fit of giggles. ... (*Shout*) "Pee pee. I have to pee pee ... I am a midwife but I am bewitched ... and I make so much pee pee ... help! ... I don't want to cause disasters ... floods ... I don't want dead men, I don't want dead men. Get me a bucket!" They gave her a bucket, she makes all her pee pee, very dignified, staring off into the

distance the way men do when they pee by the roadside.
"Give this drink to your husband. It's magic! It will move
his bowels." "Is everyone crazy in this house to think I am
going to drink the pee pee of that midwife there that I don't
even know?" "I'll introduce you, dear." "I don't want to
meet her." "But you must move your bowels." "Ah, yes,
well, throw in a bottle of Jack Daniels and some angostora
bitters, and beat up a couple of eggs in there. ... Good,
would you believe it, it's good. Want a sip?" "No, no, it's
all for you." And he drank and he drank, and his belly
swelled up and up and BOOM! ... Exploded! And of that
computer programmer not one speck was left, not even his
software that he had always kept with him for so very long.
There was the little dolly, all in one piece laughing like
crazy! "You see," she says to the grown up little girl,
"Stupid shithead. Now you're free, you're boss of your
body, your choices, your whole self— *YOU'RE FREE*! Let's
go!" The little girl hugged and hugged her dolly to her
breast until slowly, slowly the dolly disappeared right into
her heart. Now the little grown up girl is alone, walking
down a long long road ... She walked and walked, she came
to a great big tree and under that tree there was a whole
group of grown up little girls just like her. What a great
welcome they gave her! "Sit down here," they said, "Here
with us, we are all going to tell each other our life stories.
You begin, they said to a pretty little blond girl who was
there. And the little blond girl began, "When I was a little
girl, I had a rag dolly who said dirty words." "Ha, ha, ha,"
all the girls began to laugh at once, "How funny, who would
have believed it ... We all have the same story ... all of us!
The same story to tell."

BLACKOUT

DIALOGUE FOR A SINGLE VOICE

(*Let's imagine that a* YOUNG MAN *is leaning against the house opposite in a very narrow street, an alley, looking up toward a balcony or window where his* WOMAN *will appear. Finally the* WOMAN *comes to the balcony. She waves and calls to him softly.*)

WOMAN

Hey, my beautiful sweet love, hear me? I'm here ... here I am, up here! Sh-h-h-h! Don't speak out loud, don't say anything so they'll hear you.

Oh, tender beauty, forgive me if so long you had to wait before I showed myself ... oh, yes, sugar, well I know that you are upset and it is raining so hard and it seems to have fallen all on you, every drop!

But what's gotten into you? What? You're sick to death of me? But how could I help it, love baby, with my mother glued to my ass, I couldn't shake her off even if I farted! Oh, my sweet amoroso, you are so drenched, you look like a pussycat that ten old bums have pissed all over, a bunch of drunks!

No, I implore you my perfumed flower, don't force me to let you come up here to me now, because I, with this crazy desire I have for you, if I found myself together with you pasted together and tangled up, legs, arms, thighs, like braided bread ... if you tell me "I want you" I would throw down the key to you now ... But it would cause a tragedy that would make us both shit in our pants.

Be patient still a little, mio santo amoroso, you'll find the moment to come. But now it would be madness. ... My father just now came home wild like an animal ... his hands still filthy with blood, because in a fury, a swish of his axe murdered and cut into pieces the little millstone donkey because he, this naughty ass, the other night got himself loose all by himself and was riding for all the time the moon was riding in the sky the nursing filly, the horse, and certainly has made her pregnant, that bastard!

That's right, my beautiful baby, this is not a very good moment to be found naked and armed with your standard only in my bedroom ... my daddy is jealous also of me, almost as much as of his filly, and if he got suspicious that some other donkey had climbed on top of his daughter to graze like that, he would pull out, my sweet angel, with his two hands, from in between your thighs the beautiful insignia that you have brought along to make sweet war in the battlefield of my bed.

And what, are you smouldering with despair? Mio dio, what is that?

Down here, someone is coming. ... More over so he won't see you, into the little corner there, where it's darker. ... Sh, there, he's gone.

But you're so careless. I can't believe it, you've ended up under the rain spout?!!

"Acchoo."

Listen, listen, oh poor darling, how you're sneezing...!

"Acchoo."

It sounds like braying!

"Acchoo."

Stop it, behave! ... Oh, yes, I see you've caught a chill ... but I beg you, don't cough like a cigarette addict, they'll end up hearing you in the house.

"Acchoo!!"

Go away! Sail to America! ... No, no, no, no, come back, I can't do it. I can't bear to see you go. Crazy, crazy, I am ...! And you, breath of my mouth, you have made me crazy!

Oh, I like you so much, my little drowned sparrow, I have such a craving to wind you around me like a sheet and kill you with carresses and kisses, and dry you off like Magdalena with my hair ... no, only the feet ... and then warm you up with pinches and bites and squeezes ... and tickle all of you all over everywhere until finally you lose yourself to helpless laughter.

"Acchoo!"

Oh, oh, oh! Still you sneeze, my sensitive little love? Wait, let me listen a second at the room of my mother and

father if they're sleeping soundly. ... Yes, it seems that they
really are asleep. Now wait, I'll let you come up. Oh, my
swollen-up angel, my damnation ... what are you forcing me
to do ... I'm trembling all over down, down ... in my womb.
... Wait, I throw you the key; I have tied it up in my shawl.

Quickly, hurry, open ... enter, climb the stairs. ...
What are you still fussing with down there? ... How long will
it take you to put the key in the key hole? I hope so much you
will not miss finding the button hole for the button at the
right moment! ... Ah, you have done it! Close the door,
climb up quietly, Mother has the light sleep of a sexton and
for nothing she wakes up. I come to you with the light. Rise
up, rise up, my despoiler, my ruin; essence of rose. ... Embrace me!

"Oh, at last ...!"

No, don't make a noise, don't speak. Holy Mother,
you are soaked to the skin! You are worse than an icicle!

No, wait, stay away, you are too soaking wet! Couldn't
you have shaken yourself a little before coming up, like dogs
do? Look at the puddle you've made on the floor! No, no,
amore dolce, Santo ... forgive me ... I will not tease you or
scold anymore. Oh, you're right, but I beg you, don't
speak, with your deep voice you'll be heard. ...

For me, it's different ... even if they hear me talking
they won't listen, lots of times in my sleep I talk and rave all
night even. ... Come to the fire. Let me do it, I will strip off
all your wet clothes ...

"Ahch ..."

No, no, stop, don't sneeze, hold your nose, or at least,
sneeze in soprano so they'll think it is me. ... Eeeecci,
Madonna, dear sweet bimbo, I have caught your cold. ...
Shhh! Someone moved, in the other room. Hide behind the
curtain ... I'll go peek. ... No, daddy and mommy are sleeping peacefully. Come, let me embrace you. Oh, how your
heart is beating ... what is it, my Heaven on Earth, you are
shaking like the leaves of a bamboo tree. Come, come to the
fire. No, don't touch me yet with your hands, angel of my
breathing, you are like ice! ... Let me take off your shirt.

Here, lift your arms so I can pull it off and kiss your chest.
... My loved one, stretch! Forget about Daddy and his axe.
I'll put your shirt here, by the fire. ... Wait, I'll dry your
hair and stroke your back a little. ... Oh, what beautiful
skin! ... and what? You're ticklish? Don't shriek. ... It's
lucky the gentle raindrops drown the noise.

Here, a beautiful warm sheet so I can dry you. ... Let
go, stand up so I can take off your trousers. They are stuck
to you like glue. Oh, sorry, I popped a button ... here are the
trousers unbuttoned! Easy, I don't bend down, I'll do it. Sh-
sh-sh with your deep voice. ... Sit, lift one leg, this one, so I
can take them off ... why are you afraid? Even if you are
naked, on the outside you are covered better than a sultan.
... Come close so I can kiss you. Beautiful, honey, spring,
but you are burning up, do you have a fever? Oh, come
refresh your body and for me you will refresh my heart. ...
No, I'm not leaving, foolish darling, don't be frightened ...
I'm right here, I have to take off my clothes or do you want
to love me with them on? ... Yes, yes, take my clothes off me
... but gently, my rough diamond! You're zipping off my
skin! Restrain yourself! ... You remind me of a hungry little
mouse inside the cheese cellar. The shortage is over, my little mouse, it's over! Come, come, now I'm naked and
ready, come and satisfy your hunger! But be careful, don't
gorge yourself, don't rush!

Calmo! Che è? To get into the fortress you don't have
to batter down the walls. ... There's a passage slightly open
and I've already surrendered! Oh, the barbaric invader and
the Turks and the Saracen! And what? We are already
jousting?

Stop, stop! Let me breathe, truce amore! With this earth-
quake, you'll wake up the whole neighborhood! Sh-sh-sh a little ... let me listen. What's this noise? No, don't be afraid,
they're sleeping! Come, let's begin again ... but my golden
Saracen, be sweet, don't be too greedy. Cingi, cingi, breathe,
let me breathe, there's plenty of time before daybreak and a
thousand birds will be singing ... oh, swoon as if to die ... yes,
die ... dio, angelo dolce, sweeter than sugar. ...

Shh! Leave the talking to me, I'll say enough for us both! ... No, no, be still ... sweet, don't fall, don't go by yourself into those waves in that ocean ... swim with me ... don't leave me alone, I might drown.

Like on a mandolin, you play arpeggios on me, all my notes. New sounds, and flowers and laments like ballads. You are like the sea swelling with waves, swelling with wind, but never with the water never. ... God, what a beautiful animal you are! No, don't let me go, I'm falling. Hold me, angel, I'm falling. ... I'm going. ... I'm going. ... Oh, yes, moan and scream. Oh, the turbulence is big as a tempest, and there is lightning. ... Now I have seen your eyes ... and also your mouth ... take me, sweet sugar, tender flower of love, to die. ... I'm vanquished. ... My soul has left me. ... I'm going ... I'm going. ...

(*Silence, a few seconds, medieval music. The* WOMAN *wakes up suddenly.*)

Oh, mio dio, what is it? Nothing, I fell asleep and day is breaking. Neither the lark nor the cock nor any other Jewish bird had wakened me. ... Wake up, get up; sleepy love, quick, get on your feet! It's time, dear!

Come, let me put on your trousers. Oh, you're still sleepy! Lovely honeyed bandit of my love ... and the sleepy time still finds your eyes and your body is all dangling.

Come, in the bucket there is rain water, it will rinse you. Sh-sh, don't make noises and squeaks like a baby ... put on your shirt all cozy and dry. ... No, my beautiful beast of love, there is no more time to start another game, neither of tower, nor of castles. Quickly, you have to go ... hurry, and silently. Now this instant, my father wakes up and comes to wake me. ... Did you forget his custom of pulling ensigns from between the thighs of smart ones?

Hey, don't run away so quickly. ... Hello again and a kiss you want to give me before you go? And better not linger ... go, run, softly ... are you down there? ... You can leave the door open ...

(*In a loud voice.*)

Addio, beautiful love, come back tonight. You make me so happy!

Why am I shouting?

Why not? There's no danger, no one can hear. ...

Why?

Because they are not here ... no one in the house ... they are all gone from the village, to the farm.

Everyone?

Of course, even last evening, last evening and through the night. ... We were always alone. ... Ah, ah, ah. ... Fun, eh? Yes, my beautiful bewildered lover, I have tricked you!

Why? What for? Just for fun, I snared you, my strolling player. For you, fear and trembling, for me fun and games, I talking all the time and you silent. ... I the passionate one and you submitting. You all wet, and me thirsty. ...

I had to try it just once! I've always been timid when we play ... and the man above and I underneath, always caught.

This time, beautiful love: You come to screw me and I screwed you!

Addio!

BLACKOUT; MUSIC

MEDEA PROLOGUE

Here we are at the final piece* of the evening, the one that has endured the longest. It's classic, Euripides' *Medea*. We don't have to make allowances for Euripides, who was the most progressive of all the authors of Greek tragedies. He understood everything about women, about her situation, already then, and that was not just a couple of years ago.

Medea. Who was Medea? A most beautiful young woman with magic powers. She was a witch! There passed by a certain Jason, who was looking for the golden fleece. Today, people go out looking for mushrooms. In ancient Greece, everyone went looking for the golden fleece. Fleece is the hair of sheep; gold is gold! But it was difficult to capture this golden fleece, because a terrible dragon guarded it. But, Medea is a witch and ... zap, zap. With her magic powers, zam, zam, zam, they conquered the dragon. A great quarrel breaks out in Medea's family, because they don't want Jason to leave with such a precious prize. Medea sides immediately with the man who is going to become her husband; she betrays her father and murders her brother.

You ought to know, for the love of truth, that Medea was not a woman given to compromise. Then she decided to rejuvenate Jason. How do you do that? She put him to cook in a big pot and cooked away all his old age.

Every night, at this point, I interrupt myself to say to the women present, with a pressure cooker it doesn't work very well. And here, it's the first sacrifice of the woman for the man she loves. To give vigor, youth, and beauty to Jason, Medea gave up part of her youth and her beauty. They go to Corinth, get married, have two sons, and live

---

Note: It is intended that this piece be presented as the final piece of the evening, whether the entire collection be presented in one sitting or two.

happily and blessedly. How long? Alas, as is the truth for many women, as long as Medea does not begin to grow old.

Because, if between two people there is not love, that true love that is made of affection, of respect, when you begin to age, lose your sexual attractiveness, you are ready to be discarded. And for us it is hard! You are at a certain age, your children are grown, they have a life of their own, their own families, your husband looks at you—if looks could kill—and you wish truly yourself to die.

It is something to see—us women, at whatever social level, we are fragile in this situation.

The reactions we have are often a mistake, irrational. Truly it is for a woman very difficult. When you are no longer young, to start a new life, and you find yourself clinging desperately to the one you have had and then comes the humiliation, the frustration of being replaced, your substitute a woman younger and prettier: you don't want to accept it, you don't want to resign yourself. It is hard to put yourself on the shelf and pretend you don't exist anymore! It is the fastest way to lose weight that exists!

What desperation I have seen and known!

And then consider the man, who with a new love younger, loses his head. I understand it, poor things, they start to age, they discover women still like them, they are still desirable, often they truly believe it, they behave as if they are sex symbols. These couples seem so wistful: he, well turned out or not, twenty-five or thirty years older than she, at the resturant. "What does your daughter wish to eat?" Jogging, working out, always so tired, dressed "young" with a bouquet of sad rosebuds ... but saddd! And not only that, also dangerous!

Yes, don't laugh, it's a serious matter. It's dangerous; I know it. The relationship between an old man and a young girl is unfair and sometimes ... OOF! Heart attack! I don't want to frighten anyone, but it's true! Spread the word!

No one has anything against these affairs, on the contrary, every once in a while the rare one goes well even: Girls who grew up without fathers ... Yes, some go well ... for a few years. Then, inevitably, he is crying on the shoulder of an old friend and she is laughing happily with a new love closer to her own age.

The man, for an affair or whatever, can have a younger woman; the woman, no!

In fact, if a woman—let's say "adult"—has an affair with a younger man, everyone says right away, "Isn't she ashamed of herself?! What a whore!"—while for the old man with the young girl, "Wow! There's life in the old boy yet!" or "Have you seen that old fox?!"

What a shitty world. Barbaric!

And how we suffer! I think often that if our men left us for women eighty-five years old, we could understand ... we would sympathize! Poor boy ... he had a unhappy childhood ... he needs a grandmother, we would say. Instead, no, they always leave us for women younger, beautiful, stupendous!

Imagine Medea, the woman who doesn't compromise, how she responds when she finds out that Jason, without even saying, "Look, sweetheart, I'm getting married today at two o'clock," marries a beautiful and powerful young woman, the daughter of the king. The catch of Corinth. She has a fit. A Greek fit. She locks herself in her house, she cries, she hollers, she screams, then she pretends to accept her fate, and plots her horrible revenge.

With her magic powers she murders, from a distance, the future young bride and at the same time the bride's father, whom Medea also didn't like. And she's not finished yet, she also kills her own two sons. "Dear Jason, you have exploited me, humiliated me, insulted me, made me suffer mortal pain, and I return the favor, I give you the most terrible pain of all: I kill your sons."

And ZAC ZAC—they're dead. "Bye, bye!" And off she goes in a beautiful chariot that she borrowed from a neighboring king.

Tonight's *Medea*, as played in the hills of Umbria and Tuscany, is a popular Medea which follows the tragic writing of Euripides, but the statement of the reasons for killing the sons is different. This is not a drama of jealousy and wrath in Euripides. It's a matter of conscience.

In fact, Medea says a sentence, extraordinary in my view: "Children are like the heavy wooden yoke of a cow that men have put on our necks, the better to hold us down, to tame us, the better to milk us, the better to mount us. For this I kill them, to create a new woman!"

Franca Rame and Dario Fo didn't write this *Medea*. They discovered it, written in an archaic language, a dialect of central Italy.

Women audience members, it is not suggested that after you see this piece you go home and cut the throats of your children. No, this is an allegory.

We are in the square of Corinth. Here is the house of Medea. The local women, the Greek chorus, have been trying to convince Medea to come out of the house, listen to reason, and accept her fate.

MEDEA

(*Main square of the city of Corinth.*)

Ai! Ai! Ai! accorri! Accorrete! Aiuto!

Medea's locked herself in her house with her two children and she's screaming like a madwoman! She's out of her mind, like a beast, and she won't be reasonable. Her eyes are bulging out of her head as if she'd been bitten by a tarantula.

It's all a jealousy that she can't control because her man Jason is going to set up housekeeping with a younger woman. She won't be reasonable about leaving her house or giving up the children. Medea doesn't want to be reasonable.

Will you talk to her? You're the oldest.

I will talk to her because I am the oldest. ...

Medea! Medea! Come to the doorway because I must talk to you. Listen, woman, and be sensible. Not of yourself, but of your two sons you must think. How with this new marriage they're going to be situated in a much better house, in the lap of luxury, expensive clothes to wear, always bread on the table to eat, and an honored name ... and respect of the most important people for the new family: Now they're going to live in the house of the King.

For the love you have for these children, Medea, you must sacrifice. Not as a vain woman but as a worthy mother you ought to think ... for the good of your own flesh and blood be satisfied. ...

No, there is no one who has disgraced or humiliated you, your husband speaks of you everywhere with great respect and says you are the best woman, that no one is more loving to her children and to him, himself ... that always he will hold you in his heart ... What are you doing, Medea? Speak! No response? Open the door, Medea, throw in your lot with us ... who have suffered and endured the same fate, we ourselves have had wrongs done to us by our men and so we can understand you.

Back away! Medea is persuaded and comes to the door. ...
Here she is! Blessed God, how pale her face, how white
her hands. How bloodless. ...
Hold her from falling. ... Sit down on this step, Medea.
... Back away, o women ... let her breathe. We're here to
listen to you. ... Shhh! She wants to say something ... speak,
Medea. Not possible, you've screamed too much! Give her a
cup of water. ... Her mouth is so dry. Here, thus. ... Speak
now, Medea, you'll feel better if you tell us ... unbosom
yourself. ...

Women, my friends, tell me about my husband's new
woman, only from afar, once, I saw her, so beautiful and
young ... she seemed to me ... Innocent, oh, you know, I
was so beautiful and innocent when my husband first met
me. ... Long, black, shining hair and white skin, firm
breasts, so, thrusting themselves out of my blouse ... neck
without wrinkles, determined jaw, and a belly so hard and
small it was invisible under my dress. ... Sweet hips, so
delicate my whole body that when we embraced he was
frightened I would shatter ... and when he first made love to
me, his hands trembled so, his whole being trembled so,
with fear, that God would strike him down.

All of us have known that time, Medea. But the time
passes ... our destiny, the destiny of women is thus resolved:
That our men are going to seek out new flesh, and new bodies, and breasts, and an innocent voice, and new mouth
everlastingly, that's what happens, it's the law we live by!

Of what law do you speak to me, oh women? Of a law
that you my friends have thought up and discussed and written? And proclaimed, beating on the drum in the square, to
announce that it is law and binding? Men ... men ... men
against us females have thought up and written down and or-
dained this law and made it binding with the seal of the king.

No, Medea, it is nature, it is natural, the man takes
longer to grow old ... he, the man, with time ripens, we dry
up. We females swell up, then we shrivel ... he, the man
grows mature and wise. We lose our powers, he grows more
powerful. This is the way of the world.

My women, how pathetic you stand before me. Now, I perceive that man is infinitely wise having bred you to his law. ... You have submitted to his law ... to his teachings ... you have learned your lesson and you are content! You remain submissive and don't rebel!

Rebel? See, see, Medea, how you persist on giving offense to the King and to his law ... reconsider, Medea, and ask him to pardon you ... then the King will let you stay.

Stay ... stay here alone ... in this house of mine ... alone, like a corpse ... without voices, without laughter ... without love, either of children or a husband, who are already celebrating before they have buried me ... and I ought to be silent for the good of my children? Blackmail, blackmail, insidious!

Women, my friends, awful the thought that has fixed itself within my heart and mind: Kill I must my sons, thus I will be remembered by all as an unnatural mother and jealous madwoman. But better to be remembered as a ferocious beast than forgotten like a docile goat that one can milk and then despise and sell at market without so much from its mouth as a bleat!

I must kill my sons!

(*Shouting, as if to call people.*) Run, run! Medea has lost her senses! Those are not the words of a mother but of a diseased whore, a mad dog!

No, I am not unreasonable, sisters. ... I have thought and rethought then dismissed the thought. ... I have bitten my hands and beaten with stones my arms, so I would not be able to raise them to make a wound with a knife on my sons. ... First I thought to take my own life for I am not able to accept the thought of being exiled from my house, this land, this country, even though it is foreign to me ... to be loaded on to a cart and carried away the same as a prostitute, sick with mange ... because by everyone even by you more I am detested ... a pest; a deceived and complaining woman is shunned by everyone, and even by my sons when I have gone and everything will be forgotten ... disappearance as if no mother gave birth ... even Medea never born or ever loved, in no one's bed will she have been embraced, kissed or possessed. Medea dead before being born! And if it is true that I am dead and everyone has already killed me and buried me, how am I able to kill myself again? I want to live. But I am only able to live if I bring death to my sons, my flesh, my blood, my life!

Flee, flee, people! ... Medea is crazed! Flee, flee. ... Shhhh! Stop! ... Now arrives Jason, her man ... Make space there because he knows how to take care of his women ... let him pass.

Medea, look and calm yourself ... it is your husband.

Jason, what a touching idea you have had to leave your sweet bride—your perfumed and innocent rose—to come to find me! O how honest the face of the man who approaches me ... embarrassed his stride ... sorry his look. Sit down. No, don't be distressed, that for joy and amusement I feign madness ... to terrify these my dear friends, to see them running about and crying out and then laughing and laughing in the confusion. Nothing else remains for me to do to pass the time. I have come to my senses. ... Thinking and thinking through what is right: Foolish was my conceit to keep you entirely for myself ... forever ... it was the jealousy of a petty woman, as you know, weak is a woman's nature, quick to rancour, to envy, to reproach ... you must pardon me, kind Jason, for my being overcome. You have been wise to seek out new youthfulness in your bed and fresh sheets, and with people highly placed you are acquiring new relations ... and also for me you seek them, for your relations also become my relations. And I am very happy. If you pardon me I will go to your wedding ... to prepare the marriage bed with new gentian-scented sheets, more than mother, teacher I will be to the young bride in making love to please you. Are you persuaded that I have come to my senses? And to think that I called you traitor ... but man never becomes traitor if he exchanges women and a woman needs to be content to be "mother", which is already a great reward. And I thought it was a vile betrayal of our laws of men to be able to exchange ... and that this cage in which you imprison us is the worst insult! And even better to hold us women subject, our children have bound us together at the neck, chained, like the hard wooden yoke of the cow to keep us tame, to be able to milk us of our life force, and to mount us at will.

These were my thoughts, Jason ... and I think them still! And this cage of yours I want to shatter ... and this scandalous yoke, this scandalous betrayal I want to tear off!

My friends, listen as I breathe, how in one breath only, it is so great, all the air in the world I would be able to inspire.

It is necessary that these children, mine, must die because you, Jason, and your infamous laws destroy!

Arm, friends, this hand of mine. ... Plunge the knife, despearate Medea, into the tender bodies of the sons ... bleed ... honeyed confection ... bleed ... forget, my heart, that they are sons of this body ... bleed. ... And do not tremble when they scream, "Pity, Mother, pity." ... And outside the people will shout, "Monster and bitch and evil unnatural mother, Zozza." And I will say to myself, weeping (*Half voice*) "Die, die to give birth to a woman! (*High voice*) Die! To give birth to a woman!

(*The final "E" is picked up by a musical note that fades as the lights go down.*)

BLACKOUT

Monologue of a Whore in a
Lunatic Asylum

(*A* Woman *is seated on a metal chair. She has earphones on her head, a microphone before her mouth, and a series of wires that go from her wrists and ankles into an apparatus full of wires and lights that flash on and off intermittently.*)

Woman

Yes, yes, Miss Doctor, I hear you, I hear you fine. Don't be upset; I'm relaxed in spite of the fact I feel like a robot with all these wires ... in fact, I feel like I'm in the electric chair, that's the sensation ... that's it. Listen, Miss Doctor, wouldn't it be better if you come in here with me instead of staying out there in that sort-of airplane cabin? Because I can't really talk about some things unless I can look a person in the face ... while I talk ... this way I feel like I'm in a rocket taking me to the moon. I'll tell the truth just the same but I won't have to worry about all these wires and stuff. You can't? You have to stay there to control the machine? ... Okay, okay, if you can't ... then where do I start? From where we set fire to the executive offices? No? ... Prostitute? ... From when I started? Listen, Miss Doctor, I don't like to say that word there ... prostitute, I prefer to say whore, in fact, it's better to speak plainly, no?

Look, it's okay, yes, yes, I understood.

The first sexual experience. The first ... no, I don't remember it, I remember the second. ... Huh, no, the first I don't remember because I was too small ... my mother was yelling about it during a fight with my father and that's how I know that he, my father, tried to rape me ... but I don't remember it ... no, no traumatism, I liked my father. The second time ... yes, that ... I already told you. Yes, with a boy in a field behind my house. The ground was wet and my buttocks were frozen. He was a real dummy. Thirteen he

was and I twelve. For both of us it was the first time that we
did those things. We only knew babies come from the tummy. No, nothing. I didn't feel anything. Yes, I remember I
was very sore here, around my belly button. Yes, around my
navel because we thought it was there, the place we had to
make love ... he pushed his little thing in there. I told you he
was dumb ... my whole belly button was inflamed. You
know ... yes, that I know what sex is all about, uh-huh, you
can suppose that, Doctor. ... I am not a half-wit like I look
... I educated myself. I read many many books about sex ...
even scientific books. I discovered that we women have these
erogenous points, you'd say that's correct, Miss Doctor?
Erogenous ... we have erogenous points all over our bodies
... that, for me, was a revelation. I had no idea that there
were erotically sensitive spots on a woman like that. I found
a book where there was a diagram of a naked lady all divided
up into quarters ... yes, like these diagrams on the posters
that you see hanging in the butcher shop of a cow all divided
up into sections like the map of Italy divided into provinces
and districts. And each zone of the woman's body in that
book was painted with different colors according to its sensitivity, most strong to least strong on the touch of a man,
that is, when they touch it. For example, there was the loin
section, here, all painted bright red ... everyone says that's
the most sensitive. Then the part here, behind the neck, in
voilet, you know, all that part that the butchers call "the
chuck", then the "padding" of the backbone, that's the
fillet, all painted in orange dots. Then a little lower, the
rump, ah, the rump is something ... non plus ultra! Speciale
... almost like the loin ... it seems that if one knows how to
touch it correctly, the loin gives erotic tremors that explode!
Almost like touching the heart of the roast beef ... how do
you say? ... inside the thigh ... or leg?

　　See, Miss Doctor, how smart I am? I know all about the
sensuality of a woman. I do! Yes, I know it all but I'm a
half-wit, worse, an idiot, I mean deficient ... no, I'm not just
saying it to say it, no, I am someone who every so often gets
out of line ... and you know that, Doctor ... sometimes I

don't understand anything and then I do things that afterwards I don't remember. ... Huh? I know it because other
people tell me afterwards. Huh? What they tell me? ... But,
Doctor, I've already said all that to you ... ah, it doesn't
matter. I have to tell it all over again. Ah, yes, on account of
the machine that takes it down ... oh, mamma mia, I felt a
shock here! ... It's not anything? You're not going to turn
me into a roast beef, are you? Yes, yes, I'll talk.

Well, they, the others, told me that when I went out of
my head, I took off all my clothes, that I danced naked ...
that they fucked me naked ... don't say it? How should I say
it? "Took me" ... yes, they took me, but then they also
fucked me! Yes, yes, go ahead. Who? How many? Where? I
don't know. I don't remember. I know that when I woke up
here in the lunatic asylum, they had stuffed me with
sedatives and I had slept for two days running, I hurt all
over. It seems to me that they beat me up ... and, for sure,
they beat me up ... I was covered with bruises everywhere!
Even on my face! ... and what I know about it? The police
that brought me in say that I fell down. No, they did not find
witnesses. When the police arrived, it was then they took me
to the clinic, there was never anyone ... oh, if someone was
there, he just arrived or was passing by. ... But who gives a
damn ... I am a whore, no? A whore who every once in a
while has a crisis, goes crazy! But it's not that I am going into
some Greek lamentation ... you know, Miss Doctor,
because you know what everyone says: Who is a whore?
She's a person who manages to make a good living without
working! To think how I worked and how! I got a job as a
maid and they screwed me! Then I worked in a factory and
the same thing. You're stupid if you're too easy to fuck, if
they see you like it ... oh, shit! No, I don't like it! Yes, I
know it's too easy ... it's convenient to put all the blame on
the rotten men ... to blame it on society ... even my mother
told me ... if you want to be an honest woman, there's no
way, let yourself be killed, instead! In fact, I tried to kill
myself ... eight hours in the factory plus overtime ... and it's
there exactly that I went out of my mind. The first crisis I

had was at the factory: I was there a week when the hot flushes started ... my head was spinning ... but the supervisor said I was making it up, that I was complaining just to put in for benefits. So you try and you try and then I went crazy! I smashed all the windows with a dolly cart. I tipped over all the dye cans ... then I plastered the colors all over me like a painting! And then they told me I danced naked up and down the halls ... yes, I did a striptease ... right into the offices of the president with all the workers laughing at me and clapping their hands, those shits!

Huh, no, I didn't know I was doing any of it. Yes, after I went to the clinic, they made me a patient at the lunatic asylum. And when they let me out of the lunatic asylum, there was no more job ... they had fired me, the bosses. Well, listen, Miss Doctor, you can think what you want but I swear to you I am not a whore because I want to be. Look, I never found one of all the whores I know jump up and say: "Oh, it's great to be a whore!" No, they all say: "I make a little money with this lousy occupation and then I get out and get myself a little store, a little newsstand ... me and my man." If it ever came true, all the newsstands in Italy would have to be managed by whores. A doctor here, from ward fifteen, a little girl to look at her, she became my friend because I tell her everything ... and she writes it down. ... She has explained to me that when I go out of my mind, the real reason is I don't accept the idea of being a whore, that I am disturbed. ... What the hell is that to be disturbed? I tell you these things but I don't understand so much but I swear to you, Miss Doctor, that I, tell me I'm crazy. I even liked being in the factory. I had a tough time, but I was together with some women. There was so much noise, heat to make you faint, stink of the solvents that gave you a headache, the meanness of the supervisor ... but I ask myself, what, then, is it that you like about all that mess? Well, it was the respect that I had for me myself. Look, Miss Doctor, what I'm saying? If you haven't tried being a whore, you cannot understand what it is to lose respect for yourself. The rottenest thing about this occupation is that it makes you feel like a thing with a hole and legs and buttocks and teats and a mouth and that's it ... you have nothing more. And if a person's in shit, what do you do? You try to swim, not to smell the stink ... and you look for someone who will pull you up into his boat. A joy ride ... it feels like revenge: "Wanna fuck, piece of shit? Who do you think you are because you have four cents? Then pay! Fuck and pay! I'm not there. You're moaning on top but I'm not there. I pretend to be there, but I'm gone. You're fucking a dead woman, Coglione!" The fact is that in those moments there I'm gone, it's true ... and it's then that I go out of my mind ... and shame myself and dance naked ... and you and your friends in the end let loose, you slap me around ... you jump on top of me, five of you, six, you do your thing, sons of a whore ... it comes out, all the bastard hate that you have against us women. Now you feel like real men ... real bastards. But I, some real bastard that set me up the last time, I remembered: He is well-known, with a company car, office with a bar, couches, kitchen, double secretaries and real friends, pigs just like him. I pretended with me no problem ... and then I make it happen that I'm found by chance at the downstairs bar at closing time of the office where he always goes punctually like the TV news. I acted the good-time girl, already a little spacey with a friendly laugh, all freshly perfumed and looking good. There were some friends of his there making offers and he put himself in the running and I let him win: "The signore has won the fuck! Complimenti, signore!" All puffed up with satisfaction, he walks me out of the bar, winking his eyes at the guys who lost out. We go on up to his office with the adjoining bedroom and he begins his game as if they are all around, those guys from the bar to watch, jealous, and to scream "Bravo, you're fantastic, what a bull! ..." It seemed as if he had feathers even up his ass, then he collapses like a butchered cow. I got dressed and I take away with me everything I can manage: checkbook, keys to the car, to the office, to the elevator, to his house, to his garage, to his speedboat, to his safe. His passport, driving license, Rotary card, Hunt Club card,

Friends of the Red Cross card, Christian Democrats party card ... everything, even his citation for best worker in the factory hanging in a frame over his desk between portraits of the pope and the president.

I took off. I came here to this lunatic asylum. I told them I felt a crisis coming and they had to admit me. ... Ah, I forgot that before leaving, on the table in his office, I had left a note: "If you want to find me, I am in a locked ward at the lunatic asylum." The fucking bastard telephoned there to the gatekeeper where there was a nurse who knew all about it: "Ah, well! And you are the executive that has taken advantage of a sick woman." A lawyer arrived there but he, the lawyer, they threw him out. He wanted to speak to me in private but I said that, no, if he wanted to speak to me, he would have to come into the ward with all the other patients present. And when he came in, he looked like a pickled worm ... we put him on trial. He had to tell everything that with his bastard friends like him they had set me up for ten days ago. He shook ... he babbled, he cried ... "And now we will give the story to the newspapers. It is all taken down here on the tape recorder." He fell to pieces ... pudgy fool. He looked like a pig on a hook. Then we gave him back his cards and keys and stuff and sent a copy of the tape to the newspaper. He went to work like a fiend, got all his influence going, made sure that no one published a word of this whole disgusting story.

Five days later I went out through the iron gates to go home and I saw a car coming up behind me. I started to run but at the corner two guys jumped out of another car and started to beat me up so that if two nurses from the lunatic asylum who had watched everything from the gate keeper's office hadn't come flying, I would have been dead. They carried me into the emergency room more dead than alive. Then all my lunatic asylum friends carried me into the ward. They all cried, not from pity but from rage ... "Damnit!" They cried, "But is it possible that we always have to take it, get screwed, beat up, and then put up with it. We really have to do something to this bastard. ... " "It won't do any good," said the little girl doctor, "It won't do any good to try and get revenge ... it's only with an organized fight, with comrades, with politics, that you win, not with vengeance." "And who has in mind vengeance," they all said, "It is exactly political action that we want." The next night in the city a fire broke out. The building where the bastard has his office went up in flames. "Arson," said the television. "Political action," said one of the inmates. "Political action," replied all the others. The little girl doctor was quiet for a while ... then also she said, "Yes, a political act."

BLACKOUT

IT HAPPENS TOMORROW

MOELLER

They stabbed me in the heart, four times. They wanted to kill me. At the first stab I didn't scream, only a sound came out of me, like a death rattle. They threw something in my face that stunned me, ether maybe, but I managed to see them. There were three, in military uniforms. One grabbed me from behind by the hair and twisted my right arm behind my back, forcing me to sit in the chair, the other blocked my left arm and shoved his knee under my belly, forcing me to spread my legs as if they wanted to abort me. The one holding me by the hair snapped my head backwards. I saw the blade of the knife. A quick stab in the chest almost on my left breast, then a violent jerk from left to right. The blade came out. Right away a surge of blood ran down my stomach and belly. Another stab. A sharp pain, sharper than the first. This time I scream. In the wrench, when the knife comes out, I feel it scrape the ribs under my breast with a kind of screech. Another surge of blood, but not right away. Now the blood that was dripping on down, down my belly finally ran down between my legs. A rush of vomit: Something came out of my mouth, maybe it was blood ... maybe only water. The other two stabs I didn't feel. I passed out for a second. "It's done," a hard voice woke me up, "let her go." I slid down, out of the chair, and I felt myself fall hard to the floor, my face smashed against the tiles. The blood kept flowing out, a fresh surge with each beat of my heart. My left arm was still folded up under my breasts. Slowly, slowly I feel myself soaking in blood that spreads out on the floor. I was numb. The rag they threw in my face to put me to sleep was having its effect ... or perhaps it was wearing off. "It's done!" I say to myself. "It's done!" A few minutes more and then it will be over. I open my eyes wide but I can't move. I see only the crack between the tiles fill up with blood, only with one eye, the other one is in the dark, s t u c k
to the floor. I have an instinct very strong now someone is

watching me through the peephole in the door. That instinct
keeps me from moving. Slowly, slowly I try to move the
fingers of my left hand hidden under my chest at the top of
my breast bone. Yes, I succeed in moving the fingers. With
difficulty I've opened my fist. I feel the fingers soaked in a
flow of blood—that comes out through my ribs. I have found
the wide-open lips of a wound ... it's a tear. I keep on playing with it. Here's the place from which the blood is surging
out. With my index and middle finger, I squeeze very hard.
The rush of blood abates, but still so much pours out from
the other wounds, almost immediately more from above, on
my breast. The peephole in the door is still open, in fact,
noises come floating in from the corridor. The sound of hur-
ried steps, the sound of locks clicking, doors slamming.
Screams, shouts, curses, shots! "They're killing
everybody!" In the cell next to me it's Mrs. Ensslin, I hear
her scream, desperate. There's a voice giving orders.
"Make two turns with that rope, two turns! Pull now! Pull,
you two! Let's hang her up. ... Put the rope through up
there." "Up there where? There's nothing there. It all just
falls apart." The one who's giving orders swears! "They've
made these rooms too bare. At least there could be a pipe.
Pass me that little box. We'll leave them a good hook. Here,
this. Give me that, bring me that hammer and I'll knock it
inside." There are some dull thuds, then again some orders.
"Hold her legs together. Now, pull her up. Throw me rope
over the hook. Come on, now; tie, tie. Done. Let go of it.
Let's get out of here. Let's take a look at the other one."
"Wait, untie her wrists first. Now, move it. Get out, get
out."

More footsteps, more prisoners being saved, more locks
clicking, screams. Orders like dogs barking, then a shot. Dis-
tinct! Like a whiplash! The thud of a door that slams. Finally,
the remark of a voice that passes outside my cell, "It's four.
Now we can give the alarm." "No, stop!", comes another
voice, "Let's wait a little longer. In the meantime, clean up.
Pick up everything ... make a complete inspection before the
justice of surveillance and the government doctor come to

make their report. Don't leave anything around." "Open
this one, I want to take a look at Moeller. You never know."

Now, the door of my cell opens again. Sound, voices,
words now, as if through cotton, like slowed-down music.
Someone is talking from outside the wide open door.
"Christ! This one has spit up so much blood! The place is
flooded!"

"No, don't go in ... You want to slip in that puddle?
It's like walking in wet cement. You'll leave footprints, no?"
"Huh, it's useless to go in there now again. Don't you see?
She's lost all her blood!"

They close the door again. Footsteps. They open Mrs.
Ensslin's door again. "Is she dead?" "Yes, it looks it.
What's the rag? Look here, on the floor!" A second of
silence, then a barked order: "Lock up, lock up everything
and get out. We have to give the alarm!"

A succession of footsteps, people running, another
silence, this time several minutes go by. There's nobody in
the corridor. I try to move my hand, nothing, it doesn't
work anymore. I feel a tingling that goes slowly the length of
my body starting from my legs. It seems to be freezing in
here, as if I were in a refrigerated storage room. The terrible
pain in my head reverberates and reverberates. I feel as if I
have an iron pipe hammered into my neck. I'm not
breathing. I cough.

The blood comes out faster. In the corridor the alarm
rings: 10, 20 electric bells make a terrible uproar. They are
running. Some prison guards arrive. They already know where
to go. They open the four cells. They hardly pause, no one
comments. Some minutes go by, other people arrive. Then
some stretchers. Two men come into my cell. I feel everything
from a very long distance. They lift me up. I feel myself swing-
ing. They take my pulse. "No, nothing there. Her heart's split
open." "Been stabbed." "Yes, this one's dead too."

A priest entered: "Where will you take her?" "To the
morgue, all four to the morgue."

I pass by the other cells of friends who were spared.
They are closed. The doors are sound proof. They couldn't

suspect anything. And even if they did suspect, if at that moment they screamed, banged on their doors, no one would be able to hear them. Total silence.

I am dying. I hear the little bearer's voice: "There's blood dripping out everywhere. Stop a minute. Let's put on some compresses." I see them fussing around the wounds. They lift me up again. The stretcher slides around on the cart. I lose consciousness.

A burning sensation in my arm wakes me up. Someone has stuck a needle in my pulse, and a bottle of plasma is pumping in, because it goes in faster in the vein. It's a nurse or maybe a young doctor. With difficulty I open my eyes again, they say to me: "Maybe you're going to be okay! They left you for dead and they were on their way to the morgue with you. You'd lost so much blood, your pulse was already gone. This is the second bottle of plasma we've pumped in. If I hadn't noticed, you would have bled to death, stretched out on the marble slab." I try to make a smile, but it doesn't happen. I look around. There are no men in military uniforms. I make a sigh. At least I try. But I'm numb; it feels as if a rock is on my chest. They thought I was dead. That young doctor cannot conceive of the trouble he has caused the police by rescuing me in extremis.

I start again to try to smile but I stop: "Maybe they'll get rid of me before I can talk. Maybe I'll never be able to speak out. Or maybe I will." "What trouble you've caused, young man! What trouble you've caused!"

BLACKOUT

ADAPTOR'S NOTE

The concept of these adaptations is that Italian women are playing them and speaking a fluent second language. This is why an occasional Italian word is thrown in and why it is a good idea to get a sense of Italian language rhythm during the rehearsal period. If properly acted, they give the audience the pleasure of being let in on Italian women's secrets. In contrast to most theater, these pieces are specifically addressed to the women in the audience, not to the men. Don't, I beg of you, make fun of these women because you lack the courage to confront their pain and pleasure. Don't pander to the male audience. These women are deeply engaged in living and, if played that way, will be lovable, moving, and funny to both women and men.

ORIGINAL PRODUCTION

ORGASMO ADULTO ESCAPES FROM THE ZOO was originally produced by the New York Shakespeare Festival, Joseph Papp, producer. The costumes were by Ruth Morley, the lighting was by Jennifer Tipton, and the scenic consultant was Santo Loquasto.